1/16/18

– Use of lc
Why are they using π in
this way? ⌐ ~~forca~~
   1. e.g. Primitive pg. 6
   2. e.g. small ";"

NIGHT-VISION

ILLUMINATING WAR AND CLASS
ON THE NEO-COLONIAL TERRAIN

Butch Lee & Red Rover

lc
co
200/60

–Does big T Truth
   exist? pg. 9.

3 hrs
20 min

– Kahneetah
– Timberline
   – Mazamas
– Salmon
River

**VAGABOND
PRESS**

**KER
SPL
EBE
DEB**
2017

Sat
Sun ?
20 – Monday

get
to pg.
110 by Sunday night

Night-Vision:
Illuminating War and Class on the Neo-Colonial Terrain
ISBN 978-1-894946-88-9

First published in 1993 by
Cooperative Distribution Service and Vagabond Press

Many thanks to all those who worked on transcribing the previous edition of Night-Vision, thereby making this second edition possible. Work is proceeding on new material for the third edition, which will hopefully be complete soon; in the meantime this edition is being maintained in circulation by small batch print runs. Without your work transcribing, the book would be currently unavailable.

Kersplebedeb Publishing and Distribution
CP 63560
CCCP Van Horne
Montreal, Quebec
Canada H3W 3H8
email: info@kersplebedeb.com
web: www.kersplebedeb.com
         www.leftwingbooks.net

Copies available from AK Press: www.akpress.org

Printed in Canada

CONTENTS

Feel good chapter. Inspiring

pg. 13: Queer gender-bending...
reveals... how artificial
it all is

B What do you think about
the statement: "under the shifting
dunes of race, nation, & gender
there's rock..."

Inpack quote on page 14

pg 16: Melanin: the neurochemical basis for soul — discuss

pg 17: WEB DuBois:

"race has been the great issue of the 20th century, then class must surely be the great issue of the 21st century"

pg 18 — bold — discuss

Thesis?

Our predicament at the present time throws up new
questions. Neo-colonial man is asking a different set
of questions than the old colonial man. Sometimes if a
person gets trapped in a previous moment of history,
you find it hard to carry on a conversation with him or
her because they are still out to defend something that
you're not against, but you're not with because it is no
longer the relevant thing. Why should we get caught
up in making tremendous tirades against the mis-
sionaries or saying the Europeans were terrible fellows,
look at how these fellows exploited us? Why should we
continually speak in this grand singular—the African
is this and the European is the other? That was a
formulation that was necessary at a particular point
in time, when we were still within the whole identity
crisis, when we were trying to evolve a peoplehood.
But the moment we move beyond that, neo-colonial
man can't talk about the Vietnamese in the singular or
the African or the Guyanese, etc. We must look at real
life. In real life, Guyanese live in certain different ways,
have contradictions among themselves, have a relationship with the rest of the world. We must try to deal
with the resolution of those contradictions. And that is
also the case in Africa.

WALTER RODNEY

Guilt is irrelavant

- Resonated? — Thing you didn't understand
- Challenged belief

No childhood

A 9-year-old child (above) searches a garbage pile outside Quito, Ecuador, for objects he can sell, while a 13-year-old girl (left) carries cement blocks at a construction site. Thousands of children must work in Ecuador, where many people are poor and nearly half the population is under 18.

CHAPTER ONE:

DE-TOXING

Today's revolutionary need is to detox ourselves from the old, stereotyped political formulas from 20 or 30 years ago. Without which we cannot deal with neo-colonialism. A while ago i was watching a Malcolm X Day program, and the main speaker ended by militantly reciting Malcolm X's famous phrase: "The Ballot or the Bullet!" Haven't you caught the same thing? X, most fresh of all thinkers, is being turned into the equivalent of Lenin or Mao's corpse on ceremonial display. For when X threw down that slogan a generation ago, it was then timely and on point. Black people were struggling for Freedom against *colonial* conditions and most had neither the ballot nor the bullet. The militant question was which would be picked up.

Now, the Black Nation is struggling for its life against *neo-colonial* conditions and New Afrikan people have lots of ballots and lots of bullets. Everywhere you have Afrikan city governments, Afrikan officials and Afrikan executives, Afrikan soldiers, Afrikan shooters and Afrikan posses. You might say that the Black Nation is dying from too *much* ballots and bullets. But not radical enough truth, perhaps.

Under colonialism, the oppressed were largely kept disarmed. Now it's all reversed. Imperialism as a *neo-colonial system* races not to disarm (which is hopeless in this age)

but to arm the oppressed in its own way, whether it's posses
or paratroopers. Children included, naturally. Feminists say
women should get self-defense. Does that threaten imperialism? Then why is S&W making the "Ladysmith", a .38 snub-
nose specially sized for women? Is the government of white
men doing anything to stop women from owning handguns
(the ranks of white women who've done so are over 15 million and climbing)? Be real.

In the Ivory Coast and Somalia, men and boys in rags and
bare feet have AK-47s and grenades. In New York and Los
Angeles, kids too young for learners' permits got Raven 25s
or a deuce-deuce. Or maybe even a TEC-9. What's the fire-
power of the old black liberation army compared to the Crips
in Compton or to the Jamaican posses just in Flatbush? "Get
the uzi!" is successful slang because it plays off reality we all
know. More than a few New Afrikan children say personally
they got to be more afraid of Black people than white people.
So how useful is the liberal-left habit on playing low to the
crowd with old anti-colonial rhetoric?

It used to be that dissing the white man was a crime or
close to it, dangerous for sure. Life threatening if a Black
man or woman did it. Now it's so tame that Fox or ABC
gives it to us as a sitcom. There's even some college courses
on how to dis the white man. He may not like it, but who
cares (imperialism doesn't care, that's for sure). Even white
women are doing it now as a substitute for doing anything
real. It's like running in place. As Rodney, the Guyanese
revolutionary scholar, pointed out, it's counterproductive
to solving the neo-colonial situation. Revs still cling to the
old ideas and ways, in part because we don't want to admit
how ignorant we are now. This runs deeper, though. Anti-
colonial politics are the culmination of 400 years of our

struggle. They are the product of the best minds we had, of
destroying old societies, of oppressed peoples changing the
world in uprisings, pushing further and further. These old
views are already fully developed, well-honed. More than
that, the old anti-colonial politics are developed in the most
profound sense, in having been widely diffused and taken
hold of by the oppressed. Put to use already. So when revs
talk that old talk, walk that old walk, it's not only familiar
but reassuring and to a certain degree popular.

We all take for granted now the anti-colonial consciousness and changes. It's become the normal, what's our due. A
few years ago, Nelson Mandela was the most famous "terror-
ist" P. O.W. in the world. In 1990, when he made his trium-
phant visit here, he was not only greeted by massive crowds
of well-wishers but schools and churches throughout the
Black Nation held special programs to honor him. City
governments and the u.s. Congress itself had to organize
welcomes for him. Like it or not, white men had to smile
and applaud him. And last year "By Any Means Necessary"
T-shirts with Malcolm's picture on them were more common on many streets than Budweiser T-shirts, and you
can't take it to mean anything extreme or radical. The old
anti-colonial awareness has already been generalized widely,
absorbed by people & society itself into daily life. Let's break
that down.

When a tiny klan faction bused from North Carolina to
the u.s. capitol for a rally on Labor Day weekend 1990, it
took over 2,000 cops in riot gear to hold the angry crowds
back. The d.c. New Afrikan community was outraged that
any klan dared to march in their city, which is 70% Black,
on their territory. Efi Berry, then-wife of the then-mayor,
Marion Berry, came out and brought her ten year-old son,

or in 2018

too, "I'm overwhelmed," she said, "that in the year 1990 we still have to deal with this..." Although the white left organization All-Peoples Congress (aka Workers World Party) officially called the protest, put up the posters and set up the banners on the sidewalk at 15th & Constitution (where the kkk was supposed to start marching) they were never in control of the struggle.

Spontaneously, young brothers and sisters just took it over by making the action. Pushing past police and infiltrating around police lines, occupying the intersection to block the street. When a white man with a bullhorn from the International Committee Against Racism (aka Progressive Labor Party) got lured out into the street, Afrikan people got that bullhorn from him and started rallying and leading the crowd. After word spread that the klan wasn't going to show, that the cops had already cancelled their march permit and bused them direct to the Capitol building steps, the really angry crowd of 3,000–5,000 (two-thirds New Afrikan) just went right through the police lines.

It became a chaotic footrace down Constitution, as demonstrators and police in a mixed crowd ran until near the u.s. labor department building at Louisiana Avenue, where police reinforcements finally held. Out of sight, unimportant really, forty-four sorry whites of the christian knights of the kkk posed for reporters. Then got out of town, quick as possible. It's the kkklowns who are doing the running now.

The Black Nation had made its point. That people weren't going to put up with these racist insults right in their faces. Mass anti-colonial consciousness took over the scene, even without Black leaders or organization. It was a victory. "We smashed the klan!" "We beat back the klan attack!", anti-racists reported afterwards.

It showed in practice that people could confront the colonial threat, but not yet the neo-colonial threat. Handfuls of klansmen are a danger on some suburban road or by sneaking around and ambushing someone. Only a fool, however, would think they're the big threat that liberals, both white and Black, make them out to be. Does anyone dream that those 44 kkklowns could come into Flatbush or Marcy projects and push a million New Afrikans around? Intimidate folks? White hoods in the hood? The picture in your mind makes you laugh. They'd get smoked so pathetic it'd make Gen. Custer look good.

But in 1990, that same hour, the New Afrikan population of Washington d.c. was declining (which the u.s. gov says surprised them). Record numbers of Black residents with steady jobs were scattering before the fist of genocide, moving to the suburbs, breaking to Prince Georges County. Record numbers of other Black residents weren't moving out but dying out, being shot down and shot up, being imprisoned. Under a "militant" Black mayor, a Black police chief had his Black police make more than 46,000 drug arrests during the 18 months of "Operation Clean Sweep." Close to one arrest for every five New Afrikan adult residents of the city. No klan could do this. Then, to make it all kkkomplete, the Black mayor got his neo-colonial self videoed snorting coke and "womanizing." As that old Nation of Islam song went, "White man's heaven is a Black man's hell." You're still shooting blanks in a throw-down world.

The white ruling class *wants* the neo-colonial virus of Black capitalist government; it promotes, pays for and sponsors Black capitalist government. No matter what anyone's hopes were, in fact today such Black government = Black Genocide. You say something's crazy, or upside down here? Just as

Primitive : The stage that is the start of things [handwritten annotation]

imperialism not only wants to arm millions of Afrikan men indiscriminately and quickly as possible, but it's offering them a taste of everything "white" (even white women). This runs counter to all the rules of colonialism because it isn't colonialism. It's neo-colonialism, the new kid on the block. Neo-colonialism isn't any less deadly than colonialism, you know. That's why, even though it means starting from scratch, relearning, we have to understand the neo-colonial world system.

Until we put some light on the change from a colonial to a neo-colonial world, *we are locked in cycles of primitive rebellion.* We are not saying "primitive" like imperialist culture does, as a racist term implying backward and inferior, but in the true sense of those who came first, the stage that is the start of things. It took the oppressed generations to understand euro-imperialist civilization in its colonial form. To move beyond the primitive theories we first had to explain the social world. And until we did so, we were unable to defeat it.

Time after time, peoples would call on their traditional wisdom and weapons, and courageously hurl themselves against the colonial structures in primitive rebellion, to no avail. Whether it was the Indian Nations fighting back against the white settlers, or the Chinese patriots who fought to uphold their dying empire's prohibition against the British and amerikkkan opium trade, or the Ibo women of Nigeria, who in the 1915 Women's War rose up with their clubs by the thousands against the British army with its rifles, these were just but one-sided wars. Even when european armies lost battles, which they often did, they always held the long term strategic advantage. There's nothing wrong with primitive rebellion and primitive theories, mind you. It's where struggle starts.

one of largest ethnic groups in Africa   look up   oko Igbo [handwritten annotation]

At the same time, we recognize that it took generations of change to work from there to the storm of the national liberation wars, which were the high point back in the 20th century in the strategic negation of imperialism. It wasn't until revolutionary socialism led modern national liberation movements that Western colonialism as a crude system of iron handcuffs was overthrown. The revolutionary socialism of the 20th century had many faults, but it also had one historic virtue—that it was able to militarily defeat the full power of Western imperialism (that's why they hate it so badly). Not once but many times, in nation after nation. For the first time in 500 years the white man was no longer the conqueror but the loser. You can see the difference by how easily the Pentagon invaded neo-colonial Iraq thousands of miles away, but its flinch reflex about invading a Cuba only 90 miles offshore.

Now the world struggle between oppressors and oppressed is starting all over again, on new ground. What we do today relative to the present neo-colonial situation is just as primitive as those early neo-colonial rebellions. Anti-klan meetings and stoning the hasidics in Crown Heights (and the hasids are no better or worse than the klan) are as futile as going begging to the supreme court or chanting "Run, Jesse, run." These are remembered moves from anti-colonial days, which now only serve to vent anger harmlessly.

In like fashion, the search for political answers has begun again with primitive theories. For the great radical politics that once moved the lives of millions have been used up by history. Patriarchal socialism or "marxism", the old national liberation, and white feminism all lie discharged, drained, behind us in the colonial past, and no longer illuminate the road ahead.

Today the proliferation of primitive theories dominates the mass intellectual life of the Black Nation, where the tremendous pressure of Black Genocide cries for answers. The more these primitive theories veer off from the amerikkkan mainstream, of course the more interest they stir up on the street (tasting of both Revelation and forbidden fruit). From the vulgar materialist climate theory of "Ice people vs. Sun people" to Shahrazad Ali's argument that the problem is Black women's refusal to submit to her "Blackman...as the ruler of the universe and everything in it. Including the Blackwoman."

The 1960s radical Black nationalism, which was intellectually more sophisticated, exists now only as sentiment. Not as practical vision. For its dream of liberation unity had its roots, its material base, not solely in the slave experience or the Afropast, but in the modern working-class Black Nation. A community in which colonized New Afrikan people were overwhelmingly in one productive class, living one certain un-amerikkkan culture united beyond individual will. That class structure is gone with the migrating factory and the vanishing farm. As gone as the buffalo hunt. Replaced by Equal Opportunity and warlordism. Which is why young brothers and sisters have put aside those old radical programs to explore the new wave of crude and primitive political theories.

This stage of primitive theory is unable to comprehend Black Genocide, any more than a century ago the colonized peoples could at first explain the white man's superiority over all of us. One theory is that it's all a Jewish world conspiracy, while other men debate whether white men's envy of the supposedly larger Blackman penis is responsible for Black Genocide. Any flattering shallow idea that seems to

What is "true"? "Truth" *FUCK NATURAL*

come from an anti-white angle can be considered. Primitive theory also takes the shape of dead answers. Trying to grab the razor sharp neo-colonial present with old preconceptions from the colonial past. Folks reassure themselves with trueisms we never question because they seem "naturally" true or "must be" true. So while it's popular now to cry the alarm "Black Genocide!"—people still don't get it. Are still afraid to really get it.

Isn't "strengthen the Black family" the most agreed upon remedy? It's glibly proposed by everyone from Mrs. Barbara Bush to Minister Louis Farrakhan. Everyone seems to agree on that, on trying to make a future out of a better past. Yet it isn't any more real than dopehead dreams or whiskey courage. Would "strengthen the Jewish family" have saved the day in Hitler's gas chambers? Or do you believe that Cherokees died of starvation and disease on the Trail of Tears because they had single parent households? *Have* you thought about this? *ha* *yes & no*

Peoples' lips are saying "genocide" but their minds are still thinking discrimination. Trying to counter Black Genocide with old theories about racism and economics from colonial days. But our present has raced far beyond that. To not understand neo-colonialism is to not fully live in the present. Even radical Black nationalist thinking on this has gone beyond its expiration date. The river of genocide is here, now, but it's a dividing line so different from what people say.

And the struggle against the neo-colonial empire has only begun.

- Panthers
- Malcolm X?

CHAPTER TWO

REALISM OF
RACE & GENDER

Defining parameter

It's critical for us to talk about what race, nation & gender are, because this is what people are fighting about now. The main political movements—such as Afrocentric nationalism and the women's movement—are about what people think of as biology. Struggling over what is natural and un-natural for humans. Same for nations, too.

Here's a snapshot of what we mean. Last August 8th there was a rally in NYC's Federal Plaza in lower Manhattan to support the young Jamaican woman who had been the victim of gang rape in a white fraternity house at St. John's university (the rapists had been tried & found "innocent", of course). The rally had been organized by Rev. Daugherty's church and the Black Women's Center at Medgar Evers College. While everyone there was against the white rapists, it was a mix of different nations who happened to intersect at that point while going different places. Like a cultural explosion.

The first major speaker was a white woman from N.O.W., whose speech about rape was disrupted by Black activists in the crowd raising fists and chanting, "Where were you?" "Where were you?" That was a reference to N.O.W.'s daily

presence to support the young white woman victim at the
Central Park jogger rape trial, while they no-showed the
St. John's trial. But the New Afrikan sister next at the micro-
phone shouted "Where were *you?*" back at the Black men
who had been chanting, referring to the fact that few of them
had been there either until the very end. Then, the Puerto
Rican woman speaker also attacked the white women of
N.O.W. for their racist manipulation of Latinos.

All of the Afrikan men speakers linked the Jamaican
St. John's woman as a co-victim of white racism along with
the Black & Latino guys who had just been convicted of
gang raping and trying to kill that white woman jogger in
Central Park. Racism was the main issue to them.

Afrikan women speakers from the Caribbean women's
group and from Medgar Evers, on the other hand, were very
strong, linking racist violence and sexist violence as parts
of one "imperialist" culture. One of the largest contingents
there was a feminist karate group which actively teaches self
defense to both white and Third World women.

While Rev. Daugherty and other dignitaries focused on
appeals to elect more liberal "minority" politicians to make
NYC's dead and rotting government look more lifelike. Most
out of it were the male white left which seemed only interested
in their crowd vending of buttons, newspapers, and other left
archaeological artifacts. Actually, the day began with 1930s
white folksinger Pete Seeger arriving to lead the white part
of the crowd in singing their white racist song about settler-
ism & conquest, "THIS LAND IS YOUR LAND / THIS
LAND IS MY LAND / FROM CALIFORNIA / TO
THE NEW YORK ISLAND..." Not singing were Black
folks and Latins, some of whom were wondering out loud
why people were singing this white racist song.

This book is all over the place

The rally was emotional and enlightening, mixing nations with totally different futures in their present.

When well meaning people say "we're all on the same side," they just missed the train. It's a different terrain out there, more convoluted because neo-colonial *class* changes are manifesting themselves as struggles over changing race, nation & gender. Only under neo-colonialism would two Afrikan-Amerikan lawyers who share the same white values, the same white political agenda, even the same career in the same offices—be doing the Clarence vs. Anita mud-wrestling match on network television. Now white feminists love Anita, who made her career serving in a rightwing Republican administration. Is loyalty to a gender like loyalty to a race—as *both* sides really think in different ways?

class is the main divide

The backlash over that lit up a lot of things. Rosemary Bray of the *N.Y. Times* wrote afterwards: "The parallel pursuits of equality for African-Americans and for women have trapped Black women between often conflicting agendas ... Black men and white women have often made claims to our loyalty and our solidarity in the service of their respective struggles for recognition and autonomy, understanding only dimly that what may seem like liberty to each is for us only a kind of parole. Despite the bind, more often than not we choose loyalty to the race ... It has made us partners with Black men in a way white women and white men cannot know. Yet not all of us view this partnership with respect."[1]

There's resistance to seeing our races, nations and genders as being artificial, man-made and much, much more resistance to confronting the power of class to make and unmake them. But in our daily lives we know it's true; we just assume it subconsciously without really thinking about it. We think race is a biological category, although we know full well that

Juan Valdez from Colombia is *non-white* but an identical looking Juan Valdez from Spain is *white*.

When New Afrikan men speak of having "lost our manhood" under slavery, no one thinks they mean sex-change operations but everyone knows what they say is true. When a boy isn't hard enough don't the others say he's "pussy"? But they aren't thinking he grew a vagina, are they. And when Mike Tyson snarls at an opponent at a press conference, "I'm gonna make you my girlfriend!", we know what that's about. Same in the white women's community: when a woman is too outspoken, too strong, not white enough, even in the "Women's Union" they cut her, saying "She's like a man." Gender isn't about biology (that's why people go ape over gays and trans, because queer gender-bending smudges the chalked-in gender lines & reveals how artificial it all is).

We know in ordinary life these things are malleable, changeable. But when it comes to the big picture—world politics—we forget what we know. Just like we don't take "banana republics" seriously but think nations are natural communities. Wasn't there a Republic of South Vietnam (aka Saigon government), which was recognized diplomatically as a legit by the u.s.a., Great Britain, France and the other Westies? It had a million-man military & the third largest air force in the world, but they turned out to be all temps. That armored nation that was a u.s. neo-colony vanished after only 20 years of life, like a bloody soap bubble. There are TV reruns with a longer life than that. No one even remembers it.

What is really hidden is class. Because it is so feared. Everyone senses that under the shifting dunes of race, nation & gender there's rock, some massive formation underneath the surface giving us shape. What's popular is to say it's

biology. No, it's not just those persisting white guys again
with their Master Race and Mr. Gender theories. Among
others, Afrikan-Amerikan cultural nationalist intellectuals are picking up the "biology is destiny" card as well. The
racist media attacks on professor Leonard Jeffries, deposed
chairman of the Black Studies department at City College
of New York, have brought this into the news.

Dr. Jeffries believes that racial behavior, intelligence, and
especially the difference between the white race and the
darker races is biologically determined. As he said in his
weird speech at the Empire State Black Arts and Cultural
Festival at the N .Y. state capitol on July 20, 1991:

> "Ice and sun are very real and very scientific. We are
> sun people, people of color because of the sun. The
> Melanin Factor. Europeans have a lack of melanin
> and have lost a great deal of it because much of
> European development has been in the caves of
> Europe where you do not need melanin. So the
> factor of ice is a key factor in the development of
> the Europeans biologically, culturally, economi-
> cally, socially. And what we are talking about is the
> values that are transmitted from ecologies."[2]

These aren't wildly eccentric views, as the white press likes
to say, but really conformist views. People absorbed by euro-
capitalism are trained to mis-think of class roles as only biological destiny, as race or gender.

White science said for centuries that because of excess
melanin, because of un-natural genetic selection in a hot &
unhealthy tropics, that the Black race was not fully human.
Jeffries is only using the same eurocentric crackpot concepts, although with different motives. This trend has been

Reverse "eugenics"

catalyzed by rap groups and religious groups—i.e. the righteous teachers—and is considered by many searching for a deeper Afrocentric answer.

Dr. Jeffries, as he always is at pains to point out, isn't a lone voice and hardly originated these ideas. Dr. Frances Cress Welsing, M.D. described the white race as albinos whose "true status as a recessive genetic mutant" of the real humans, the Black race, accounts for their evil nature. We can easily recognize this as a secularized plagiarism of the Dr. Yacub legend in the Honorable Elijah Muhammad's teachings.[*] Dr. Cress Welsing continues her secularized recycling of the Nation of Islam's gospel in theorizing that the naturally high levels of melanin in Afrikan skin give superior & even superhuman abilities:

inverse of "eugenics"

> "The Cress Theory of Color Confrontation and Racism (White Supremacy), links whites' unjust behavior towards people of color (black, brown, red and yellow) to whites' inability to produce melanin skin pigment in the skin melanocyte. The whites' numerical minority status in the world and, ultimately, their fear of global white genetic annihilation by the genetically dominant, skin melanin producing, non-white world majority are pointed out as additional reasons for white aggression towards people of color. This thesis helps explain the evil 'kill or be killed' behaviors of the global white collective in relation to non-white people.

Nation of Islam

---

[*] While the cosmology of the N.O.I. is in any factual sense untrue, it is no more fantastical or fictitious that the teachings of the Old Testament, Judaism, Christianity, Hinduism, or other faiths eurosociety deems respectable. *True dat*

"In 1972, I presented a paper entitled, *Melanin: The Neurochemical Basis for Soul*, at the annual meeting of the National Medical Association Section on Neurology and Psychiatry. I theorized that the presence of melanin in high concentrations in Blacks accounted for some of the observable difference in behavior between Black and white people (i.e., religious responsiveness, rhythm, emotional responsiveness, sensitivity levels) ... hehe

"Fifteen years ago in a paper entitled, "Blacks, Hypertension and the Active Skin Melanocyte" (*Journal of Urban Health*, 1975), I posited melanin, among other things, as a possible neurotransmitter and the skin melanocytes as the foundation of the sixth sense—the basis for knowledge of the unseen, including a deeper knowledge of 'bad.' ...

"In 1987, at the first Melanin Conference, I discussed The Cress Theory on the George Washington Carver Phenomenon, suggesting that the skin melanocytes of this very Black-skinned scientist (high level concentration of melanin skin pigment) enabled him to communicate with the energy frequencies emanating from plants. Thus, he was able to learn their secrets and purposes."[3]

Catch this contradiction: While the pop fusion of pseudo-biological politics and imaginary race history seems zany and more than a little pathetic in the age of lasers and real biotechnology, it flowers precisely because the oppressed world is searching, groping for a deeper answer than the old 1960s radical politics that didn't work. A deeper answer into

searching ... groping

themselves, into their identity as a race, nation & gender. Most of all, the oppressed want to know why they keep losing and why they can't make things work.

It's too easy to understand colonialism only on one level and not to understand neo-colonialism at all. Just as we have only a stereotyped idea of what class is. Here "marxists" are usually among the worst offenders. You know, the stereotyped fantasy of heroic factory workers making revolution against the Rockefellers. Well, that won't cut it. Not against neo-colonialism, which is a much more sophisticated system of oppression. And it certainly won't cut it in the u.s.a., which is the most highly developed neo-colonial society in the world (one where white workers want & vote for the *Trump!* Rockefellers to be their leaders). Neo-colonialism is a system that takes many more forms than capitalism did before. As Amilcar Cabral said thirty years ago, neo-colonialism *its* represents an imperialism that can take the form of anti- *insidious* colonialism or even of "socialism" if need be. Even back then, *flexible* Cabral foresaw the need to bombard old stereotyped politics.

If it is as W.E.B. DuBois said, that race has been the great *was* issue of the 20th century, then class must surely be the great *race* issue of the 21st century. The hold of race & nation & gen- *just* der on political affairs is because they have a dual power: of *a mask* their surface identity, physically & biologically, and of their *for* deeper power as indirect forms of class, as how class mani- *class?* fests itself through these building blocks of human culture & identity. This is the insight modern revolutionaries discover and rediscover in each time and place.

Frantz Fanon pointed out how colonialism compressed society's economic structure and cultural superstructure into one—"you are rich because you are white, you are white because you are rich,"[4] he wrote. It is the truth of human society not only that class struggle is the motive force of history, but that the dominant classes, the great classes, in their rise must of necessity take over & redefine gender, nation & race to their needs.

marks

Just as the early euro-amerikan capitalists took a class relationship, that is a hierarchical structure of economic roles & property relations, between themselves and their slave proletarians, and gave it the outward clothing of race. In class society what is man-made is always disguised as the natural, the biological, or the Holy. What we think of as race or gender or nationality is class in drag.

We don't mean that these categories are illusions. Far beyond their physical bases, they're real enough to get killed for & real enough to determine your life from infancy to old age. They're intensely real in our identities. Folks get up front & personal real fast over questions of their race, their gender & even their nation. We all know that. What gives these social categories such raw power isn't biology or nature. No, the reverse. What's so compelling is that these are the cultural roles that people construct to bind society's needs & decisions down into everyone's personal identify where it becomes daily life.

It follows inescapably then, that what is "natural" to race, to gender & nation keeps changing, evolving just as class does, as society develops and new needs and conditions emerge. In modern times, the ruling class decides what gender, race & nation are, while the oppressed fight back by liberating and redefining for themselves these building blocks of human culture.

This isn't difficult to catch. When we hear the word "farmer" we picture a man. You don't say "Bob, the male farmer", while it's common to hear "Bob, the male nurse."

Because here farmer is "naturally" male and nurse is "naturally" woman. Yet, the u.n. says that ⅔ of the world's food production is by women. In many societies, women as a gender equals the people who grow the food. Women are historically the farming class, to put it another way.

But as soon as capitalist development infects agriculture, with farming as a cash export business, then the ruling class reassigns land and farming to men as part of their gender identity. This isn't dead history. It's a transformation going on right now in tribal areas of India, in Zimbabwe, throughout the neo-colonialized Third World. Everywhere women are being driven off the land—and Nature has nothing to do with it. Weren't we once told by euro-capitalist culture that farming was naturally male (allegedly because of their physical strength), while being confined to unpaid domestic work in the house was natural to women? Neither role was ever "natural" in the slightest, of course, as we know by the truth that they never applied to the Afrikan women & children who with Afrikan men actually did the back-breaking labor of growing much of amerikkka's most profitable crops for centuries.

In that sense, Afrikan women have always been defined by settler amerikkka not merely as less feminine, but as not being women at all. Existing as neither male nor female in white amerikkkan culture, Black women have been treated as being without human gender. As Toni Morrison has said, Black women have been viewed by amerikkka as part work animal and part reproducing machine. Which may be why in 1992, without thinking twice, so many liberals say that "Black men are an endangered species," a species apparently with only one gender. Words betray meanings folks don't even admit to themselves.

In amerikkka's 19th century crisis over race, gender &
nation, which they call the Civil War between North and
South, even many white anti-slavery men argued that biological destiny had given to the white man those characteristics
of superior reasoning & enterprise that made him the ruling
race, the ruling gender, and the ruling nation. (amerikkka
was created as a nation of white men, with women & slaves
as their property) Afrikans were like white women, it was
said, in that their natural abilities were in the areas of intu-
ition and emotion. This could allegedly be seen in their
superiority in gospel music, religious fervor, and sexuality.

The preeminent amerikkkan anthropologist of that time,
Harvard's Louis Agassiz, told President Lincoln's Freedman's
Inquiry Commission that he believed it wasn't "safe" to let
Afrikan men have political power, because they were, in
his words: "indolent, playful, sensual, imitative, subservient,
good-natured, versatile, unsteady in their purpose, devoted
and affectionate."[5] Just what capitalism had ordered women
to be in the dominant judeo-islamic-christian ideology.

In "The Negro," his famous speech before the 1863
American Anti-slavery Convention, white abolitionist editor Theodore Tilton scoffed at prejudice against the Afrikan
man just because of his different mental ability. Tilton, as
a "friend" of the Negro, pointed out how unreasonable this
was, since the woman-like Afrikan man could not fairly be
compared to the born-to-rule, truly masculine white man:

> "In all those intellectual activities which take their
> strange quickening from the moral faculties—pro-
> cesses which we call instincts, or intuitions—the
> negro is the superior to the white man—equal to
> the white woman. The negro race is the feminine

race of the world ... We have need of the negro for his aesthetic faculties ... We have need of the negro for his music ... But let us stop questioning whether the negro is a man ..."[6]

This is what the "friends" of New Afrikans were saying back then. If this then-liberal explanation sounds truly insane to us now, it only illustrates how ruling classes continually manipulate what is race, gender & nation—which as social categories are ever-changing and plastic to the human will. Of course, if you went up to Mr. and Mrs. Clyde B. Kop at the shopping mall & told him his wife reminded you of a feminine Afrikan man ... well, you might have to start ducking lead. But you notice that white men & their institutions still pair up white women & New Afrikan men—as the two politically important "minorities", as the sexually forbidden conspirators in their fantasies. Although those 19th century phrases are too culturally revealing to be used today, the Afrikan race is still considered "the feminine race of the world." There are many levels of meaning in this.

So there's a question: if New Afrikan men ("indolent, playful, sensual, subservient ... unsteady in their purpose") were supposed to be the natural equal to white women, what then were the even-lesser New Afrikan *women* equal to? A century has brought many things to fruition, but amerikka has never wanted to answer this. Every day we run into this unanswered question—say, in Spike Lee's films, or in the media fix on "Black men an endangered species" (that odd species with only one sex), in the attempted white feminist ownership of Black women's identity. But we're getting ahead of ourselves.

Not only is amerikkka infighting over all this right now,

but be careful that white women don't co-opt feminism [handwritten annotation]

but so are former colonies like New Afrika. The biggest issue in the Black community isn't race, it's gender. Because so many people understand that one will determine the other. *Same with white men.* The biggest right-wing white movement isn't overtly over race, it's over gender; because they believe that the future of their race (and nation) depends on who controls women's gender.

happening / class warfare [handwritten annotation]

They're even speaking of a possible civil war among whites. Michael Bray, the famous anti-abortion leader & clinic bomber, openly speculates: "Maybe we will have abortion states and abortion-free states. That may be a solution to avoid the same scene as the Civil War."[7] i.e. white men's states & "others" states.

A fight to decide what races, genders and nations mean exists because national liberation movements won on the world scene & forced decolonization. We're going to break this down starting with race and gender and working our way to nation.

MADE IN THE "U.S.A."

Our very concept of race was invented by Western capitalism to meet its needs. The so-called white race, for instance, was invented right here in the u.s.a.—the very concept of a supposed white race wasn't big in european history.

Until recently, europeans both here and there didn't view themselves as belonging to any one race. Speaking different languages and having different historical origins, often at war with each other and even appearing to have physical differences (Sicilians, Swedes, Jews and Poles certainly didn't look alike), europeans customarily considered themselves as being of different races. Of course, what they meant traditionally by race was closer to what we now mean by saying a People. Both the Italian word "razza" and the German "rasse" meant breed or tribe (by that usage every Indian Nation or european nation could be a separate race).

So when the English settlers here spoke of a superior white race they only meant their so-called "Anglo-Saxon race" from the British isles. Irish immigrants were said by them to be inferior beings of the unstable "Celtic race." It's revealing that what we recognize as nations they thought of as races.

As was pointed out in the book *Settlers*, even as late as the 1930s & 1940s it was widely believed in amerikkka that most europeans were not "white" but of very different and even inferior races:

> "The St. Paul, Minnesota District Attorney argued in Federal court that Finns* shouldn't receive citizenship papers since 'a Finn ... is a Mongolian and not a "white person."' Scientists were prominent in the new campaign. Professor E.A. Hooton of Harvard University claimed that there were actually *nine* different 'races' in Europe, each with different mental abilities and habits. As late as 1946, in the widely-used textbook, *New Horizons In Criminology*, Prof. Hooton's pseudoscience was

hu'h

---

* Finland is a small Northern european nation on the Baltic Sea between Sweden and Russia.

quoted by police to 'prove' how Southern Italians
tended to 'crimes of violence,' how Slavs 'show a
preference for sex offenses,' and so on."[8]

We're familiar, maybe too familiar, with white racism, with
its program for the superiority of the white race. But we can
miss the main point by assuming that the white race is itself
a natural thing. The white race thinks a certain way no matter how many years we scrub-a-dub-dub their minds with
civil rights, for the same reason that a dope dealer's pit bull
strains to attack, because they were deliberately constructed
that way. As a race. CONDITIONED

there it is again

For a minute don't worry about that race-*ism* and concentrate on that race-*reality*. There's nothing natural about these
races. They didn't just happen 'cause of moms or by accident
or evolution. Capitalism actually *created* Races from different peoples, put them together as specified communities to
be parts in its colonial system. And they were consciously
remade or even eliminated to meet capitalism's needs. That's
what is happening all over again today, as capitalism trans-
forms our world to enter the neo-colonial age. That's what
we're confused about.

Think about it. The entire Western Hemisphere is pop-
ulated with new races that didn't exist before colonialism.
Unconsciously, we know all that in the back of our minds,
but we should put the meaning together.

It's easiest to start with Latinos, the supposed "Brown"
race. There wasn't a single one on the face of the earth before
1492. Before colonialism wiped out many of the different
native societies of Central & South Amerika, raped and
enslaved the survivors, then forced them to adopt a common
euro-language & euro-religion. Physically, what amerikkka

calls a race ranges from those of purely Afrikan ancestry and those of purely european ancestry, to those of Indigenous or Indian ancestry and all points in between. So how can this race be about genetics?

Nor was there a Black race before 1492. It isn't true that New Afrikans in the u.s. are like the Afrikans they used to be. How could they be? Colonialism took Afrikans of many different tribes, peoples & empires, who had different cultures, looked different, and spoke different languages, and transported them to capitalism's New World across the Atlantic. Here they were forced to fuse into one people, with european, Indian and Latin infusions, intermarry, adopt the English language & religion, forge a new culture for themselves, and take on new class and gender roles as an internal colony within a european settler empire. Capitalism defines them as a race, as a biological and "ethnic" group, because they don't want to concede that in that historic process a new society, a Black Nation was formed, with all the human rights to self-rule and sovereignty that that implies.

The necessities of the colonial system pushed for the invention of the white race. Not merely as master race propaganda to justify colonialism, but as constructed social reality. Liberals have always said that people took something natural—the white race—and made up stereotypes about its being superior. That's missing it. Capitalism *made* the white race, constructed it socially, economically, culturally & even biologically. Artificial but real. Dr. Frankenstein is a metaphor in lit for something that really happened.

For amerikkka, capitalism needed to recruit every person who was vaguely european to their settler occupation force, so as to keep the Indian Nations and the enslaved Black Nation under guard. So starting with English colonies, where the master race was defined as the so-called "Anglo-Saxon race" from England, the growth of amerikkka into a settler-colonial empire dictated an equal growth in the master race to include more & more europeans and semi-europeans of different nationalities. The criminal society that they created to enforce colonialism was code-named the white race (aka "America").

Just as—to put it in perspective—the German nazis insisted on calling their rival criminal society the "Aryan race." In both cases, genocidal national empires led by capitalism created race as a mass class structure for maximum criminal solidarity, to hold territory, to conquer rivals. As Adolf Hitler remarked: "What does it matter that the communists want to nationalize a few factories? I will nationalize the entire People!"[9]

That millions of Germans were willing to kill & kill for this so-called Aryan race (the whiter-than-white detergent race that biologically doesn't exist) made it a powerful social reality in the world. That's just as true in "democratic" Germany today, which is Aryan still. And isn't it the same with amerikkka's white race? If you left it to a white majority there would be a Fuhrer in Louisiana right now.

Nations, like races & genders, have been created in capitalist history to carry out roles, to have class functions. Under colonialism, "Nations became almost as classes." The New Afrikan Nation was created to be a proletarian colony, wholly owned by but *alien* to parasitic amerikkka. The New Afrikan Nation was put together to be like a class itself, a captive nation of producers. We are going to go into this, the making of the white nation or race and the making of the New Afrikan Nation or race as two opposed *class*-civilizations.

"By the time of the settler War of Independence,
the Afrikan nation made up over 20% of the non-
Indian population—one Afrikan colonial subject
for every four settlers. Afrikan slaves, although
heavily concentrated in the plantation colonies,
were still represented throughout the settler territories. Their proportion in the non-Indian population ranged from 2–3% in upper New England to
8% in Rhode Island, to 14% in New York, and to
41% and 60% respectively in Virginia and South
Carolina. While they mainly labored as the agricultural proletariat, Afrikan labor played a crucial
role in all the major trades and industries of the
times. The colonized Afrikan nation, much more
than the new Euro-Amerikan settler nation, was
a complete nation—that is, possessing among its
people a complete range of applied sciences, practical crafts, and productive labor. Both that colonized
nation and the Indian nations were self-sufficient
and economically whole, while the Euro-Amerikan
invasion society was parasitic. While the class
structure of the New Afrikan nation was still in a
formative stage, distinct classes were visible within
it well before the U.S. War of Independence.

"In Virginia, it appears that an overwhelming
majority of the skilled workers—carpenters, ship
pilots, coopers, blacksmiths, etc.—were Afrikans.
Nor was it just nonmarket production for direct
use on the plantation; Afrikan artisans produced
for the commercial market, and were often hired
out by their masters. For example, we know that

George Washington was not only a planter but also
what would today be called a contractor—building structures for other planters with his gang
of Afrikan slave carpenters (the profits were split
between 'The Father of Our Country' and his slave
overseer). The Afrikan presence in commerce and
industry was widespread and all-pervasive, as one
labor historian has summarized:

"'Some of the Africans who were brought to America in
chains were skilled in woodcarving, weaving, construction, and other crafts. In the South, Black slaves were
not only field hands; many developed a variety of skills
that were needed on a nearly self-sufficient plantation. Because skilled labor of whatever color was in
great demand, slaves were often hired out to masters
who owned shops by the day, month, or year for a
stipulated amount. Some were hired out to shipmasters,
serving as pilots and managers of ferries. Others were
used in the maritime trades as shipcaulkers, long-
shoremen, and sailmakers. A large number of slaves
were employed in Northern cities as house servants,
sailors, sailmakers, and carpenters. New York had
a higher proportion of skilled slaves than any other
Colony—coopers, tailors, bakers, tanners, goldsmiths,
cabinetmakers, shoemakers, and glaziers. Both in
Charleston and in the Northern cities, many artisans
utilized slave labor extensively.'

"Afrikans were the landless, propertyless, permanent workers of the U.S. Empire. They were not
just slaves—the Afrikan nation as a whole served
as a proletariat for the Euro-Amerikan oppressor

nation. This Afrikan colony supported on its
shoulders the building of a Euro-Amerikan society
more 'prosperous,' more 'egalitarian,' and yes, more
democratic than any in semi-feudal Old Europe.
The Jeffersonian vision of Amerika as a pastoral
European democracy was rooted in the national
life of small, independent white landowners. Such
a society had no place for a proletariat within its
ranks—yet, in the age of capitalism, could not
do without the labor of such a class. Amerika
imported a proletariat from Afrika, a proletariat
permanently chained in an internal colony, laboring
for the benefit of all settlers. Afrikan workers might
be individually owned, like tools and draft animals,
by some settlers and not others, but in their colonial subjugation they were as a whole owned by the
entire Euro-Amerikan nation."[10]

The productive New Afrikan Nation's polar opposite was
the "United States", which from its inception was a criminal
society of parasites. This isn't racism we're talking about. The
u.s.a. was a specific type of nation, a white settler empire: a
nation whose male citizens were imported garrison for an
invading euro-capitalism; a nation whose only territory is
the Land they conquered & cleared by genocide; a nation
that is really an empire containing many captive nations
on the continent & abroad. And lastly, a nation whose race
knowingly agreed to be oppressors & mass murderers in
return for a higher standard of living and the "right" to be
parasitic on other peoples. This is what shaped the content
of their character, as a civilization. *Settlers* says:

[handwritten marginalia: "ugh", "so sick of this"]

"The key to understanding Amerika is to see that
it was a chain of European settler colonies that
expanded into a settler empire. To go back and
understand the lives and consciousness of the early
English settlers is to see the embryo of today's
Amerikan Empire. This is the larger picture that
allows us to finally relate the class conflicts of settler Euro-Amerikans to the world struggle.

"The mythology of the white masses holds that
those early settlers were the poor of England, con-
victs and workers, who came to North Amerika in
search of 'freedom' or 'a better way of life.' Factually,
that's all nonsense. The celebrated Pilgrims of
Plymouth Rock, for example, didn't even come
from England (although they were English). They
had years before emigrated as a religious colony
to Holland, where they had lived in peace for over
a decade. But in Holland these predominately
middle class people had to work as hired labor for
others. This was too hard for them, so they came
to North Amerika in search of less work and more
money. At first, according to the rules of their
faith, they farmed the land in common and shared
equally. Soon their greed led them into fighting
with each other, slacking off at assigned tasks, etc.,
until the colony's leaders had to give in to the settlers' desires and divide up the stolen land (giving
'to every family a parcel of land').

"This is typical of the English invasion forces. A
study of roughly 10,000 settlers who left Bristol
from 1654–85 shows that less than 15% were

proletarian. Most were youth from the lower middle classes; Gentlemen & Professionals 1%; Yeomen & Husbandmen 48%; Artisans & Tradesmen 29%. The typical age was 22–24 years. In other words, the sons and daughters of the middle class, with experience at agriculture and craft skills, were the ones who thought they had a practical chance in Amerika.

yuppie

"What made North Amerika so desirable to these people? Land. Euro-Amerikan liberals and radicals have rarely dealt with the Land question; we could say that they don't have to deal with it, since their people already have all the land. What lured Europeans to leave their homes and cross the Atlantic was the chance to share in conquering Indian land. At that time there was a crisis in England over land ownership and tenancy due to the rise of capitalism. One scholar of the early invasion comments on this:

"'Land hunger was rife among all classes. Wealthy clothiers, drapers, and merchants who had done well and wished to set themselves up in land were avidly watching the market, ready to pay almost any price for what was offered. Even prosperous yeomen often could not get the land they desired for their younger sons … It is commonplace to say that land was the greatest inducement the New World had to offer; but it is difficult to overestimate its psychological importance to people in whose minds land had always been identified with security, success and the good things of life.'*

land = housing/ real estate

que es?

"It was these 'younger sons,' despairing of owning land in their own country, who were willing to gamble on the colonies. The brutal Enclosure Acts and the ending of many hereditary tenancies acted as a further push in the same direction. These were the principal reasons given on the Emigration Lists of 1773–76 for settling in Amerika. So that participating in the settler invasion of North Amerika was a relatively easy way out of the desperate class struggle in England for those seeking a privileged life."[11] [...]

jump

"The essence is not the individual ownership of slaves, but rather the fact that world capitalism in general and Euro-Amerikan capitalism in specific had forged a slave-based economy in which all settlers gained and took part. Historian Samuel Eliot Morison, in his study of *The European Discovery of America*, notes that after repeated failures the Europeans learned that North Amerikan settler colonies were not self-sufficient; to survive they needed large capital infusions and the benefits of sustained trade with Father Europe. But why should the British aristocracy and capitalists invest in small family farms—and how great a trade is possible when what the settlers themselves produced was largely the very raw materials and foodstuffs they themselves needed? Slavery throughout the 'New World' answered these questions. It was the unpaid, expropriated labor of millions of Indian and Afrikan captive slaves that created the surpluses on which the settler economy floated and Atlantic trade flourished.

helping hand

just business

"So all sections of white settler society—even the
artisan, worker, and farmer—were totally dependent
upon Afrikan slave labor: the fisherman whose low
grade, 'refuse fish' was dried and sold as slave meal in
the Indies; the New York farmer who found his market for surpluses in the Southern plantations; the
forester whose timber was used by shipyard workers
rapidly turning out slave ships; the clerk in the New
York City export house checking bales of tobacco
awaiting shipment to London; the master cooper in
the Boston rum distillery; the young Virginia overseer building up his 'stake' to try and start his own
plantation; the immigrant German farmer renting
a team of five slaves to get his farm started; and on
and on. While the cream of the profits went to the
planter and merchant capitalists, the entire settler
economy was raised up on a foundation of slave
labor, slave products, and the slave trade.

"Nor was it just slavery within the Thirteen
Colonies alone that was essential. The commerce
and industry of these Euro-Amerikan settlers
was interdependent with their fellow slave-owning capitalists of the West Indies, Central and
Southern America. Massachusetts alone, in 1774,
distilled 2.7 million gallons of rum—distilled from
the molasses of the West Indies slave plantations.
Two of the largest industries in Amerika were
shipbuilding and shipping, both creatures of the
slave trade. Commerce with the slave colonies of
not only England, but also Holland, Spain, and
France, was vital to the young Amerikan economy.

> Eric Williams, Walter Rodney, and others have
> shown how European capitalism as a whole literally
> capitalized itself for industrialization and World
> Empire out of Afrikan slavery. It is important to
> see that all classes of Euro-Amerikan settlers were
> equally involved in building a new bourgeois nation
> on the back of the Afrikan colonial proletariat."[12]

In amerikkka, class has always in the long run determined
race, nation & gender (not for individuals, of course, but on
a larger scale for peoples). When the mass industrialization
of the North began, the laborers and "industrial helots" were
largely european immigrants—but they were categorized
as "non-white" and weren't u.s. citizens.* Until well into the
20th century the "dago" from Italy, the "hunky" from Poland
and Hungary, were not white in the Northern cities. "White"
meant Northern european & particularly Anglo-Saxon
English.

It wasn't until WWI, when u.s. imperialism expanded
across both oceans to become a world power, that the ruling class decided that these "non-white" races of lower-class
europeans needed to be transformed into loyal white amerikans. Only then were they raised up from semi-colonial status, given better jobs & wages, homes, education and white
status. The racial makeup of u.s. capitalism's white race was
not actually decided until then, two centuries after the occupation of this continent first started.

---

* Helots were the slave class of the legendary military city-state of
Sparta in ancient Greece, where free men did no labor but only fought
wars. That was the popular term amerikkka used for its new industrial
workers.

"The industrial system in the U.S. came into full
stride at the turn of the century. In 1870 the U.S.
steel industry was far behind that of England in
both technology and size. From its small, still
relatively backward mills came less than one-sixth
of the pig iron produced in England. But by 1900
U.S. steel mills were the most highly mechanized,
efficient and profitable in the world. Not only
did they produce twice the tonnage that England
did, but in that year even England—the pioneering center of the iron and steel industry—began
to import cheaper Yankee steel. That year the
U.S. Empire became the world's leading industrial
producer, starting to shoulder aside the factories of
Old Europe.

"Such a tidal wave of production needed markets
on a scale never seen before. The expansion of
the U.S. Empire into a worldwide Power tried to
provide those. Yet the new industrial Empire also
needed something just as essential—an industrial
proletariat. The key to the even greater army of
wage-slaves was another flood of emigration from
Old Europe. This time from Southern and Eastern
Europe: Poles, Italians, Slovaks, Serbs, Hungarians,
Finns, Jews, Russians, etc. From the 1880s to the
beginning of the First World War some 15 millions
of these new emigrants arrived looking for work.

"In 1910 the U.S. Immigration Commission said
'A large portion of the Southern and Eastern immigrants of the past twenty-five years have entered
the manufacturing and mining industries of the

eastern and middle western states, mostly in the capacity of unskilled laborers. There is no basic industry in which they are not largely represented and in many cases they compose more than 50 percent of the total numbers of persons employed in such industries. Coincident with the advent of these millions of unskilled laborers there has been an unprecedented expansion of the industries in which they have been employed.'

"In the bottom layers of the Northern factory the role of the new, non-citizen immigrants from Eastern and Southern Europe was dominant. A labor historian writes:'More than 30,000 were steelworkers by 1900. The newcomers soon filled the unskilled jobs in the Northern mills, forcing the natives and the earlier immigrants upward or out of the industry. In the Carnegie plants of Allegheny County in March, 1907, 11,654 of 14,539 common laborers were Eastern Europeans.'

"This new industrial proletariat—the bottom, most exploited foundation of white wage labor—was nationally distinct. That is, it was composed primarily of the immigrant national minorities from Southern and Eastern Europe. Robert Hunter's famous expose, *Poverty*, which in 1904 caused a public sensation in settler society, pointed this national distinction out in very stark terms:

"*In the poorest quarters of many great American cities and industrial communities one is struck by a most peculiar fact—the poor are almost entirely foreign*

Slum/ghetto

*born. Great colonies, foreign in language, customs,
habits, and institutions, are separated from each other
and from distinctly American groups on national and
racial lines ... These colonies often make up the main
portion of our so-called "slums". In Baltimore 77 percent of the total population of the slums was, in the
year 1894, of foreign birth or parentage. In Chicago,
the foreign element was 90 percent; in New York,
95 percent; and in Philadelphia, 91 percent ...'*

"Even in an industry such as steel (where the work
week at that time was seven days on and on), the
new immigrant workers could not earn enough to
support a family. In 1910 the Pittsburgh Associated
Charies proved that if an immigrant steel laborer
worked for 365 straight days he still could not provide a family of five with the barest necessities.'

key

"And these were men who earned $10–12 per week.
In the textile mills of Lawrence, Massachusetts, the
15,000 immigrant youth from age 14 who worked
there earned only 12 cents per hour. A physician,
Dr. Elizabeth Shapleigh, wrote:'A considerable
number of boys and girls die within the first two
or three years after starting work ... 36 out of every
100 of all men and women who work in the mills
die before reaching the age of 25.'

"In the steel mill communities—company towns—
these laborers in the pre-World War I years were
usually single, with even married men having been
forced to leave their families in the'old country' until
they could either return or become more successful.

They lived crowded into squalid boarding houses, owned by 'boarding-bosses' who were fellow countrymen and often as well the foremen who hired them (different nationalities often worked in separate gangs, so that they had a common language.)

"Sleeping three or four to a room, they spent much of their free time in the saloons that were their solace. As in all oppressed communities under capitalism, cheap drink was encouraged as a pacifier. Immigrant mill communities would fester with saloons—Gary, Indiana had more than one saloon for every one hundred inhabitants. Of course, the local police and courts preyed on these 'foreigners' with both abuse and shakedowns. They had few democratic rights in the major urban centers, and in the steel or mining or rubber or textile company towns they had none.

"In the U.S. Empire nationality differences have always been disguised as 'racial' differences (so that the Euro-Amerikan settlers can maintain the fiction that theirs is the only real nation). The Eastern and Southern European national minorities were widely defined as non-white, as members of genetically different (and backward) races from the 'white' race of Anglo-Saxons. This pseudoscientific, racist categorizing only continued an ideological characteristic of European capitalist civilization. The Euro-Amerikans have always justified their conquest and exploitation of other nationalities by depicting them as racially different. This old tactic was here applied even to other Europeans.

"So Francis A. Walker, President of M.I.T. (and the
'Dr. Strangelove' figure who as U.S. Commissioner
of Indian Affairs developed the Indian reservation
system), popularized the Social Darwinistic theory
that the new immigrants were 'beaten men from
beaten races; representing the worst failures in the
struggle for existence ...' Thus, as double failures
in the 'survival of the fittest,' these new European
immigrants were only capable of being industrial
slaves.

"The wildest assertions of 'racial' identity were common. Some Euro-Amerikans claimed that these
'swarthy' Europeans were really 'Arabs' or 'Syrians.'
U.S. Senator Simmons of North Carolina claimed
that the Southern Italians were 'the degenerate
progeny of the Asiatic hordes which, long centuries
ago, overran the shores of the Mediterranean ....'

"A widely-read *Saturday Evening Post* series of 1920
on the new immigrants warned that unless they
were restricted and kept segregated the result would
be 'a hybrid race of people as worthless and futile as
the good-for-nothing mongrels of Central America
and Southeastern Europe.' On the street level,
newspapers and common talk sharply distinguished
between 'white Americans' and the 'Dago' and
'Hunky'—who were not considered 'white' at all.

"The bourgeoisie had a dual attitude of fearing these
new proletarians during moments of unrest and
eagerly encouraging their influx when the economy
was booming. It was often stated that these 'races'

were prone to extreme and violent political behavior that the calm, business-like Anglo-Saxon had
long since outgrown. One writer in a business
journal said: 'I am no race worshipper, but ... if the
master race of this continent is subordinated to or
overrun with the communistic and revolutionary
races it will be in grave danger of social disaster.'

"One answer—and one that became extremely
important—was to 'Americanize' the new laboring masses, to tame them by absorbing them into
settler Amerika, to remake them into citizens of
Empire. The Big Bourgeoisie, which very much
needed this labor, was interested in this solution. In
November, 1918, a private dinner meeting of some
fifty of the largest employers of immigrant labor
discussed Americanization (this was the phrase
used at the time). \ Brazilifization

"It was agreed by those capitalists that the spread of
'Bolshevism' among the industrial immigrants was
a real danger, and that big business should under-
cut this trend and 'Break up the nationalistic, racial
groups by combining their members for America.'
It was thus well understood by the bourgeoisie that
these European workers' consciousness of themselves as oppressed national minorities made them
open to revolutionary ideas—and, on the other hand,
their possible corruption into Amerikan citizens
would make them more loyal to the u.s. Imperialism.

"The meeting formed the Inter-Racial Council,
with corporate representatives and a tactical

window-dressing of conservative, bourgeois 'leaders' from the immigrant communities. T. Coleman DuPont became the chairman. Francis Keller, the well-known social worker and reformer became the paid coordinator of the Council's programs. It sounded just like so many of the establishment pacify-the-ghetto committees of the 1960s—only the 'races' being 'uplifted' were all European.

"The Council also, in concert with government agencies and private capitalist charities, promoted Americanization 'education' programs (i.e. political indoctrination): 'adult education' night schools for immigrants, state laws requiring them to attend Americanization classes, laws prohibiting the use of any language except English in schools, etc., etc. The Americanization movement had a lasting effect on the Empire. The Inter-Racial Council was dropped by the capitalists in 1921, since by then Americanization had its own momentum."

What jumps out at us is how euro-capitalism used its mass construction of different races to disguise nationality differences & even deeper than that, class difference. This isn't merely a trick: race is the class, is the nation. "White", after all, is in its essence a class. A meta-class, if you want. As we heard earlier, in the 1920s Finnish immigrants, of all people, were among those singled out for "racist" attacks, declared non-white, persecuted by police and deported by thousands. Because Finnish workers then were too oppressed and too politically anti-amerikan to be "white". Most were young immigrants who didn't speak English, poor timber workers and miners and mill workers.

These un-amerikan Finnish workers were saying they ought to take care of the bosses with rifles, just as they had in overthrowing the Russian Czar (Finland had been a Russian colony until 1917). When a communistic party was first started in the u.s. in 1920, *forty percent* of its members were Finns. Capitalists thought this was a "communistic race" for sure, definitely not white. Only after mass arrests, mass deportations by la migra, and repression of the Finnish community could they gradually become white.

Before 1492 there wasn't even an Indian race (so named, after all, only because dummy Columbus thought he'd discovered India in Asia when he ran into the Caribbean). There were over 300 different native societies in the Western hemisphere. Speaking different languages, having different economies & cultures, ranging from urban empires to small fishing tribes. They didn't consider themselves a race back then, but only different peoples.

Indians never united against the British or the Spanish precisely because they weren't a race. They didn't consider themselves any closer to other native peoples than to these new european peoples. That's why there wasn't an American Indian Movement back then but there is now, now that they've been given a common language, a common "res" experience, a common situation—and have been made into a race by euro-capitalism.

Races are neither just natural biological groupings nor are they just fiction. Liberals used to pretend that race was "only skin deep": only about unimportant skin color and hair differences blown up by prejudice. It's not like that. Capitalism created its races out of different peoples as building blocks of its culture, to carry out different assigned roles, as meta-classes.

A PREREQUISITE: EMPTY THE CONTINENT

The situation, then, that Indians found themselves in was not exploitation or racism as amerikans think of it. Indian civilizations were forced into a unique role: to die off. "The only good Indian is a dead Indian," white pioneers always said. De-populating the hemisphere of its original societies was & is fundamental to world capitalism; it's what made "America" possible (aren't euro-amerikans only the people Adolf Hitler wanted to be?) So u.s. capitalism hasn't even wanted to exploit Indians in wage labor.

Their economic role as a race has been to become extinct. Settlers notes:

> "So the early English settlers depicted Amerika as empty—'a howling wilderness,' 'unsettled,' 'sparsely populated'—just waiting with a 'VACANT' sign on the door for the first lucky civilization to walk in and claim it. Theodore Roosevelt wrote defensively in 1900: '...the settler and pioneer have at bottom had justice on their side; this great continent could not have been kept as nothing but a game preserve for squalid savages.' ...

> "Amerika was 'spacious' and 'sparsely populated' only because the European invaders destroyed whole civilizations and killed off millions of Native Amerikans to get the land and profits they wanted. We all know that when the English arrived in Virginia, for example, they encountered an urban, village-dwelling society far more skilled than they in the arts of medicine, agriculture, fishing—and

government.* ... There was, in fact, a greater population in these Indian nations in 1492 than in all of Western Europe. Recent scholarly estimates indicate that at the time of Columbus there were 100 million Indians in the Hemisphere: ten million in North America, twenty-five million in Central Mexico, with an additional sixty-five million elsewhere in Central and Southern America ...

"Conservative Western historical estimates show that the Spanish 'reduced' the Indian population of their colonies from some 50 million to only 4 million by the end of the 17th century.

46 million

"And from the 10 million Indians that once inhabited North Amerika, after four centuries of settler invasion and rule there were in 1900 perhaps 200,000–300,000 surviving descendants in the USA ...

"So when we hear that the settlers 'pushed out the Indians' or 'forced the Indians to leave their traditional hunting grounds,' we know that these are just code-phrases to refer politely to the most barbaric genocide imaginable. It could well be the greatest crime in all of human history. Only here the Adolf Eichmanns and Heinrich Himmlers had names like Benjamin Franklin and Andrew Jackson.

---

* The first government of the new u.s.a., that of the Articles of Confederation, was totally unlike any in autocratic Europe, and had been influenced by the Government of the Six Nation Iroquois Confederation.

"The point is that genocide was not an accident, not an 'excess,' not the unintended side-effect of virile European growth. **Genocide was the necessary and deliberate act of the capitalists and their settler shock-troops.** The 'Final Solution' to the 'Indian Problem' was so widely expected by whites that it was openly spoken of as a commonplace thing. At the turn of the century a newspaper as 'respectable' as the *New York Times* could editorially threaten that those peoples who opposed the new world capitalist order would 'be extinguished like the North American Indian.' Only a relative handful of Indians survived the time of the great extermination campaigns. You see, the land wasn't 'empty' after all—and for Amerika to exist the settlers had to deliberately *make* the land 'empty.'"[13]

This is what makes Indians as a race so unique. It isn't that all Indians are extinct, obviously. *But to capitalism they are, in a certain sense. A race of survivors, remnants by the capitalist way of looking at things, from murdered civilizations and still captive nations.* You can see this in the cultural reaction to the Indian protests over the legitimization of white racist slang and the white exploitation of Indian names, images & symbols. Euro-amerikans just don't get it. They "love" Indians, they think. amerikkka loves the "natural" and "untamed" and "savage" symbolism of their Indians as a race. Perfect to name trucks and consumer products after. They're dead civilizations, so what does it matter? They're part of natural history now, like neanderthal or animal species. You don't ask dolphins what they think of "Flipper", do you?   hehe

Indians point out that calling a football team "Washington

Redskins" is ok in the nation's capital, but no one even considers having a "Detroit Niggers" or "Miami Cuban Faggots" because these refer to "real" living peoples who would be offended. While Indians are safely gone as far as capitalism is concerned.

A.I.M. leader Clyde Bellancourt notes that if Ted Turner is serious when he says that calling his baseball team the "Atlanta Braves" shows respect & honor, then he should just call them the "Atlanta Jews," instead. Turner could replace the team's "Chief" cheerleader, who wears an Indian costume with a feathered religious headpiece, with a "rabbi" cheerleader in full religious garb who blows the shofar every time a "jew" hits a homerun. And instead of the fans waving their foam rubber tomahawks—the supposed Indian symbol—in the Atlanta "chop" to spark off a rally, they could all put on black beanies and wave dollar bills—the supposed symbol of the Jews.

Having been so close to being wiped out, Indians as a race have been removed in the capitalist mind from the list of real human societies, and are now just historic cultural exhibits there for the mis-using. To capitalism (and its white servant race), the reservation equals art museum plus zoo. Isn't it interesting that even white feminists are asserting their Master race privilege to appropriate whatever they want of Indian women's lives & cultures. It's a fad among white lesbians to take Indian-sounding names for themselves, and to kidnap Indian children to "adopt" so they can own a family too. White feminists are freely plundering Indian women's jewelry, their textile designs, their ideas, their story, even concocted versions of their spirituality. Don't think this is racism, because for white women this is our race. And isn't it our gender, too?

— Dual boot

Understanding that race was politically constructed by capitalism to carry out class roles, then it's just another step to see that the same goes for gender. Capitalism's ingrained mindset that these things are somehow naturally determined, biologically fixed, is hard to break. Race & gender have biological roots, of course. White men's science says today that race properly refers to the three biological divisions of the human race—divisions they call "caucasoid", "mongoloid", "negroid"—based on minor physical differences of skin color, hair, blood type distribution, facial features & proportion of bones.

Of course, they didn't believe that yesterday and they may not believe it tomorrow. In any case, these minor physical differences are only a reference point for the vast superstructure of race that world capitalism created. Who else could have done it?

We say race involves *minor* physical differences because the truly *major* physical difference among humans exist at the further reaches of the sexual spectrum. Bio speaking, Clarence Thomas is more like David Duke than he is like Assata Shakur (culturally, too).

And although so called sexual differences among folks ain't as clear cut as most of us have been taught, we'll use the term *Gender* to mean those differences in behavior, social role & characteristics of women and men in a given society.

When european capitalism reshaped gender under its rule, they did so around class & race. White women were to be unnaturally "feminine"—which meant physically weaker, delicate, dependent, "lily-white", housebound, caretakers to men, and "alluringly" satisfying to male domination. Only upper-class women and women from the middle classes, the Lady & the Housewife, could truly become these artificial women, of course. By definition, colonial and lower-class women were excluded, had failure to gender, we might say.

Race became gender. For the making of the white race involved the politicized un-making of women to fit into "white." euro-capitalism artificially remade its women physically weaker, domestic & dependent.

Catherine is the main woman character of Zola's novel, *Germinal*, written in 1885 and based on true accounts of French miners' lives (and an actual mining disaster). When the reader first meets her she is getting up to begin another work week:

> "Catherine made a desperate effort. She stretched, and clenched her hands in her reddish hair tangling over her forehead and neck. Thin for her fifteen years, she was wearing a tight-fitting chemise that exposed only her bluish feet—which seemed to be tattooed by coal—and her delicate arms ... She put on her miner's trousers, slipped on her coarse cloth jacket, fastened her blue cap over her piled-up hair ... On leaving Village 240, Catherine had taken the main road into Montsou. Ever since the age of ten, when she had begun to earn her keep in the mine, she had run about the countryside alone, enjoying the complete freedom customary in mining families ..."[14]

Etienne, the young laborer who is the novel's protagonist, is hired as a coal hauler for Catherine's work team:

> "The young man, whose eyes were becoming adjusted to the dark, studied her. Her skin was still a sickly white; he couldn't really be sure about her

male gaze

age, but she was so frail that he guessed her about
twelve. Yet she had a boyish freedom and a naive
impudence that he found somewhat disturbing,
and he sensed that she must be older. He did not
find her attractive... But what surprised him most
was the strength of this child—a nervous strength
in which there was also a great deal of skill. With
rapid and regular shovelfuls, she could fill her cart
faster than he filled his, then push it to the incline
with one slow, smooth motion, passing easily under
the low rocks. He, on the other hand, bruised himself terribly, ran his cart off the rails, and become
hopelessly stuck."[15]

Catherine was not a fantasy heroine, the princess waiting for
her frog (the idea that if you have sex with a frog he'll turn
into a prince for you was just a clever ad campaign by Joey
Isuzu—in real life, you just got fucked by a frog). Nor was
she a "role model," feminist or otherwise. Catherine wasn't
"feminine" because she was still a woman—strong physically
and morally, not parasitic on colonialism, productive & self-
supporting. Exactly the gender that euro-capitalism needed
to eliminate to make a white race. And they did. White
women aren't like that.

  In the early decades of colonial Virginia's plantation (i.e.
koncentration kamp) economy, european women who were
indentured servants labored without freedom or wages
in the fields alongside Afrikan and Indian slaves. Worked
and lived together. Since "like is drawn to like," there were
in the 1600s european-Afrikan Nations, marriages, and
even working joint escapes to sanctuary with the Indian
nations, and even working class rebellions. In 1663 there

was an Afrikan-Indian-european slave revolt in that colony. That's no way to start a Master race to loyally administer colonialism.

divide people up

— So european women were taken out of the fields, given lighter work, and freed from bondage earlier (indentured servants were given ship passage to the colonies in return for a specified term of years in unwaged labor to a master). New laws made it a crime for european women to have sexual relations with Afrikans, and specified that any children of such relationships would be taken from the mother & made slaves. In other words, european women were made "white".

And in Zola's novel *Germinal*, on Etienne's first day on the job as a hauler—a job traditionally done by women and girl-children—he is greeted by a miner's contemptuous observation: "So, the men are taking the bread away from the girls now!"[16] In the late 19th century, French capitalism was forcing women out of the coal mines, as part of the program of "protecting" (i.e. making dependent & defenseless) women whose gender was being remade. They, too, were colonized, but in a different way.

Gender can even drift away from sex, away from its physical moorings. Sometimes Western cattle ranches had not enough women, and white men had to substitute other men to serve them. In popular culture, these men then became viewed as having feminine characteristics. Recall those Chinamen cooks in the Western movies? The ones always called "Charlie" or "Hop Sing". Notice how hollywood portrays them as not-men, like substitute women. They show no interest in sex or white women. They just want to stay home and serve the white man, cooking his hot meals and washing his clothes. They seldom take part in men's conversation, only occasionally giggling or making simplistic

All over the damn place

East of Eden

remarks. In the movies, "Charlie" is childishly loyal to the white rancher, but of course completely alien to his manly affairs. All around him rage wars, genocide, Indian treaties, rape and land deals are going on, but that's "men's bizness" and not his. Just like the "good woman." Race becomes gender, in the necessity of class.

Everyone's discussing this now, what's the hidden truths of race, nation, gender & class? *Newsweek* has a cover story, "Was Cleopatra Black?" Gays & lesbians demand legal marriage status, to register each other with the state just like they register their cars. White women managers are claiming that being of the "touchie feelie" gender makes them better capitalist executives than men. And children are getting in the action, too. A new "anti-achiever," lower-class cartoon kid who flips off adult authority is a fad: "Don't have a cow, dude." A character whose cartoonist creator assumed was *white*, whose actual skin color in the cartoons is *yellow*, but who Afrikan kids perceptively insist is really *Black*. White men "just don't get it." So if we're discussing what it all means, if it's all in flux, how can these things be fixed or "natural" or biological?

There's a fluidity, an interpretation, between race, nation, gender & class. A deeper relationship we're only starting to try & understand. They aren't separate totally, like four houses on a block. Or even like four sides of one house, although that's a better analogy. They influence & evolve with each other, even taking on each other's characteristics. Oppressed peoples have been chipping away, fighting to open up and redefine these building blocks of colonized culture for generations.

CHAPTER THREE:

THE MAKING OF NATIONS

Growing up at a time when national liberation movements dictated the firefights of world politics, we nevertheless haven't thought much about nations themselves. Now neo-colonialism has placed heavy stress along the national fault lines of the u.s.a., making its future shape as a nation uncertain. Some people go around opposing nationalism as inherently oppressive. They don't want any nations over them, and oppose the State as anti-freedom. They particularly don't want male nations hanging over them.

Other people go around *wanting* a nation, so they can get out from under their oppressors. The only way they see to govern themselves is to control a space, a territory, have their own nation. Both viewpoints are true.

Start with colonialism: in its most general sense, colonialism is defined as the conquest & ownership of one people or country by another. As such, it has obviously been around a long time. While colonialism in that broadest sense is not a class structure but a process, it has been the DNA out of which class structures have grown. In the modern age, people usually use the term to specifically refer to the system of Western capitalism & its colonial empires.

So we have to view the duality of colonialism, as both the Western capitalist system and all the earlier oppressions—such as those of women and other submerged peoples—that led up to it.

Colonialism, which in general obviously long pre-dated capitalism, is the source of capitalist industrialization and thus of modern Western culture. From it alone came the capital investment and the kkkulture to build the industry, military, and technology that gave the West world supremacy. This is not a discussion of the past so much as it is the future. Stay tuned.

The intellectual representatives of capitalism duck & dodge on this. They want us to believe that the breakthrough to scientific civilization was generated *within* whitesville, by white entrepreneurial profits, by white technology. White "marxists" have said the same thing in different terms, saying that industrialization came from white people ruthlessly exploiting the white working class. Karl Marx himself, of course, wrote more than once that the world-shaking rise of industrial capitalism was completely based on Afrikan slavery. Without which, he said, capitalism would have suffered "the total decay of trade and of modern civilization."

It wasn't until modern anti-colonial movements began that the relationship between colonialism and capitalist development began to be investigated scientifically—by the oppressed. An example out of many: In 1943, the West Indian historian Eric Williams (later to be prime minister of decolonized Trinidad) wrote *Capitalism and Slavery*, a landmark study which proved that British industrialization was created by the Afrikan slave trade. He told how James Watts' invention of the steam engine that was the breakthrough power source for the West's factories, railroads and ships, was financed by slave traders. In his brilliant study, Williams explained how the British automobile industry, their giant

Lloyds and Barclays banks (still among the world's largest),
and even the affluent & supposedly pacifist Quakers who
began those banks were financed by the immense profits of
the Afrikan slave trade.[17]

Radical feminist theoreticians, in particular the circle
around German sociologist Maria Mies, have reached back
even further and excavated the colonial roots of Western
capitalism in the conquest & ownership of women. What
Maria Mies, in her groundbreaking book, *Patriarchy and
Accumulation on a World Scale*, calls the "inner colony." The
significance of what they've done is that their insights are
the "missing link", connecting up the inner life of patriarchal
european culture to the outer life of capitalist world conquest, from feudalism to neo-colonialism. The difference in
this angle of insight is an even more radical cut on how capitalism, beneath its veil of profits & wages, runs on genocide.
As a structural necessity, as its daily fare. To quote from the
first chapter of *Women & Children in the Armed Struggle* [re-
printed in The Military Strategy of Women and Children,
published by Kersplebedeb in 2003], an Amazon Nation paper that embodies this new critique of Western capitalism:[*]

> "Genocide is itself a basic economic activity, what
> lies behind commodity production under the
> capitalist system. Genocide, i say, begins with the

---

[*] Readers who have seen the original chapter will realize that this
quoted passage, lengthy as it is, is an abridgement that barely does justice to the thesis. Further, that although the authors of this informally
distributed non-academic paper do not cite sources, it is obvious that
their analysis of european history is based on the ideas of Maria Mies'
Patriarchy and Accumulation on a World Scale. Even many historical
examples, such as the medieval case of Bailiff Geiss of Germany, are
actually quoted from Maria Mies' work.

global wiping out of women's society and women's economy, and the resulting slave labor of hundreds of millions of women and children.

"Euro-capitalism first arose through the era of the Witchhunt—the institutionalized terror against women in Western Europe that lasted over 500 years, from the 12th through the 17th centuries. Women accused of being witches were arrested and tortured by the authorities until they confessed to being agents of satan.

"The total number of women imprisoned, tortured and/or killed by the Witchhunt was in the millions. One German prosecutor alone, Benedict Carpzov of Saxony, signed 20,000 death sentences of accused women in his career. In the patriarchy's history books all this is trivialized as a bit of religious hysteria or merely a colorful case of how ignorant people were back then.

"What is real is that the Witchhunt was a *social institution*, in which the killing of women was tied to the birth of euro-capitalism. This is how our amerikkka began, in the first 'Right to Life' movement.

"Women were attacked in so violent a way not because of feudal backwardness, but because of the needs of the new capitalism gradually being born within the old European society. The patriarchy's Witchhunt was in the first place directly economic, a means of unwaged capital accumulation. Special bodies of armed men seized women's property to help finance the growth of nation-states.

"There were many independent women in feudal
society. Craftswomen weaving silk and other fine
textiles, small street merchants selling produce and
handicrafts, women farmers. In some cities women
had their own guilds (early form of unions) of artisans. Endless royal wars over land and trade routes
had left numerous widows with small houses,
perhaps a shop or other property. And peasant
families, unable to feed all their children, sent their
girl-children away to the cities to find their own
livelihoods as artisans, prostitutes or peddlers.

"It was independent women who were the main
targets of the Witchhunt. When Catherine Hernot,
postmistress of the German city of Cologne, was
burned at the stake as a witch, it was because a
powerful family wanted a monopoly on the lucra-
tive postal business. Unmarried women, who were
not owned by a man, were a majority of those
burned as witches, with widows being 40–50% of
the victims.

"In the Witchunt all the property of arrested
women belonged to the State, with the court
system taking part of the loot as fees to the male
lawyers, bailiffs and soldiers. But the lion's share
of this wealth minted from slaughtering women
went to the State treasuries. It paid for the armies
of men who produced nothing useful, for highways
to carry trade, for expeditions to 'discover' the Third
World—in short, the pre-conditions for capitalism
to grow.

"In unwaged capital accumulation from the looting of outlawed and marginalized people, Europe was learning the methods that it would use in colonialism. Women were euro-capitalism's first colony, the 'inner colony' as European radical feminists have termed it.

"It wasn't superstition, then, but cold, cold business that led one German official, bailiff Geiss of Lindheim, to write his lord for permission to kill a new batch of women (just think of him as ollie north or ed koch and you'll know him):

"*If only your lordship would be willing to start the burning, we would gladly provide the firewood and bear all other costs, and your Lordship would earn so much that the bridge and also the Church could be well repaired. Moreover, you would get so much that you could pay your servants a better salary in the future, because one could confiscate whole houses and particularly the more well-to-do ones.'*

"It wasn't just that cash, however. No, they had to do it. The Witchhunt was real to them because there really were 'witches' they had to hunt down—radical women and women seeking knowledge forbidden to us.

"Rebellion against the corruption took many forms. One that involved many thousands of women was the movement of voluntary poverty. That was a social and political struggle in religious form.

"Beginning in the 13th century women called
Beguines appeared, living communally in groups
of women's houses and wearing hooded robes of
grey or black. They supported themselves by handicrafts or begging (from the Beguines and their
male counterparts, the Beghards, come our present
words, 'beggar' and 'begging'). Some wandered from
town to town as vagabonds, preaching a kind of
theology to other women.

"Voluntary poverty was not a renunciation of the
world to Beguines as it was to many medieval nuns,
but a means to revolutionize the world for women
escaping the patriarchal family. Beguines said that
the acquiring of material wealth was an absolute
evil. Owning any individual property, even jewelry
or numerous changes of clothing, was considered
wrong.

"Beguines didn't marry. In fact, many of them
upheld the right of people to freely have sexual
relations without sin. That was a radical idea for
women in that age. As was their insistence on
women educating themselves and writing their own
religious doctrines.

"Those women were not just critics of the feudal
order, but were trying to organize women and men
into an alternate culture against the encroaching
capitalism. As part of the heretical socio-religious
movement of 'the Free Spirit', they said that no
one who was in the upper classes was without sin,
while the oppressed classes were the sole bearers of
righteousness.

"Beguines numbered in the hundreds of thousands, primarily in France, Belgium and Germany. In the German city of Cologne alone there were 2,000 Beguines by the 13th century. They came to this culture of voluntary communalism and poverty from every class: craftswomen and widows of merchants, urban workers and former peasants.

"In some medieval cities a certain neighborhood would become the women's quarter, with most houses occupied by Beguines and other independent women. One historian estimated that the Beguine community in the city of Strasbourg, France, was at least 10% of the total population.

"Beguines were a non-hierarchical people, with each house making its own rules, electing its own leaders, and deciding its own finances. Many Beguine houses were led by peasant or working class women, in contrast to Europe's growing class barriers. The Beguine women's communities were really the only democracy anywhere in Europe.

"While early feudal society, like Rome and Greece before it, saw women as lesser beings and the rightful property of one man or another, the emerging euro-capitalist order categorized women first as a natural resource of the nation-state. Biological factories like forests of timber and herds of meat. And this was as capitalist development itself was causing chaos, forcing migration and abandonment of the old ways, and as more women were rebelling. The Witchhunt was meant to destroy women as

a people, so that the capitalist nation-state could
rise up.

"White women still take all this with a grain of salt,
as the saying goes. These are merely tales of the
bad old past, which can be safely appreciated as
comforting proof that 'you've come along way, baby!'
'Cause it's so different for us now. In one generation we got women astronauts and women execs,
women paratroopers and women mayors. Not only
sex discrimination lawsuits, but Gerry and Martina,
too.

"What's it mean, then, to talk about the Witchhunt
and genocide against women? White feminists
today like to identify with the 'witches.' That's what
i mean, we don't know who we are. We aren't the
'witches.' We are the ones on the other side: the
loyal sisters and wives of the euro-men doing the
policing and burning. The sisters of patriarchy
trying to protect themselves from the terrorism by
submitting, trying to be the unthreatening helpers.

"We were taught to join Dick in doing genocide, lest
we, too, be his victims. After generations of conditioning and bribing, we follow Dick's rules as a
reflex, without even noticing.

"One big rule is cover up genocide: never see it,
never admit it.

"The impact of expanding Europe on what is now
called the Third World was supposedly a colli-
sion of advanced whites and undeveloped colored

people, of euro-capitalism's superior science and economic power overwhelming primitive tribes. But in 1492, when Christopher Columbus' expedition ran into the Caribbean islands, Europe was not advanced over the nations of Asia, Afrika, the Middle East and the Western Hemisphere. Its technology and economy were different, but not advanced or superior. It's that difference that we gotta focus on.

"In many respects, euro-civilization was both technologically and economically backward. Europe was known as a poor barbarian region isolated on the periphery of the trade routes between the world's main civilizations.

"I know this is hard to believe, because everyone just 'knows' that for whatever reasons, modern science and industry first came into being in Europe and settler amerikkka of the mid-1600s.

"There are British-trained physicians, men representing the most advanced medical science that euro-capitalism had. But they didn't seem to be able to do anything about smallpox, the most feared contagious disease of the times. Not only did smallpox, a viral infection, exterminate whole Indian communities, but it continued to kill and disfigure thousands of white settlers.

"White people did notice, though, that many of their Afrikan slaves didn't get smallpox even in the midst of epidemics. This was puzzling to the white doctors.

"Of course, the reason that some Afrikan slaves didn't catch smallpox was that they had been immunized as children in Afrika, or had been secretly immunized in the slave quarters. For in the region of West Afrika that most slaves came from, smallpox was known and a crude inoculation against it was already known (using pinpricks to transfer some clear serum from a smallpox sore to the body of an uninfected person; what resulted was milder infection producing the antibodies that gave lifelong immunity to smallpox, although some still died from the crude inoculation). All slaves who knew were sworn not to tell Europeans.

"So who was backward and who had the advanced medical technology? Just because they were captives, laborers kept in rags, didn't mean that Afrikans had no science. Even though their science had to be practiced as a conspiracy.

"Afrikan slaves here were party to scientific knowledge that was shared by most of the world: with the Han empire in China, with Arab civilization, with Greece and Turkey, with the physicians of the Moghul empire in India (who are thought to have used smallpox inoculation since 1000 A.D.). Except in areas where the disease was rare, such as in the Western Hemisphere, the major civilizations of the world knew—but not backward Europe.

"Afrikan slaves had been secretly using smallpox inoculation for almost a century, before amerikkkans found out how to do it. And again, it

wasn't any white male physician with his degrees
and bank accounts who learned. It was a woman to
woman transfer of science. British feminist Mary
Wortley Montagu learned about inoculation from
Turkish women (she was married to the British
ambassador to the Ottoman empire, though for her
it was only an escape from an arranged marriage).
In 1717 she wrote her friend, 'Mrs. S.C.':

> "'I am going to tell you a thing that will make you
> wish yourself here. The small-pox, so fatal and so
> general amongst us, is here entirely harmless by the
> invention of ingrafting, which is the term they give it.
> There is a set of old women who make it their busi-
> ness to perform the operation every autumn, in the
> month of September, when the great heat is abated...'

"In that same year Mary Montagu demonstrated
smallpox inoculation on her son, and by 1721 it
was being tried, with great controversy, by the
medical patriarchs of England. There was much
fear and superstition about this vaccine among
white society, ordinary as it was to the rest of the
world.

"Public fears about smallpox inoculation reached
the point of hysteria in the amerikkkan colonies.

"Even though the campaign for smallpox inoculation was led by Cotton Mather, the greatest of the
New England Puritan ministers and the man who
had earlier led the campaign to root out the hidden
nests of 'witches' among white women.

"Mather himself was attacked, and his home firebombed, during the inoculation controversy of 1721. Mather stuck to his guns because his Afrikan slave, 'Onesimus,' had advised him that all the slaves knew that inoculation did work, and that he, 'Onesimus,' had been inoculated himself as a child in West Afrika.

"The science of what is now called the Third World was still leading and teaching the backward European civilization.

"There's a barbed point inside all this.

"When we strip away the mystique of euro-capitalist technology, we find that it runs on genocide. And it had its origins in conquest, not in the thrown-out musing of Greek philosophers. euro-capitalism didn't colonialize the world because of its superior sciences and industry. That proposition has things upside down. Only from its ever expanding conquests and genocide of other peoples and nations, did euro-capitalist civilization slowly gain the scientific and economic superiority that we now assume is only right and natural.

"Genocide is itself a material economic force; not mere racism, but the productive center, the heart of the new euro-capitalist world order. It took all the wealth violently squeezed out of the European laboring classes for centuries just to keep the ruling aristocracy, the Church, and the rising merchant-capitalists going; to pay for their luxurious lifestyle, their waste and speculation, and the always high

cost of their wars and their parasitic State appara-
tus. On top of that, to build factories and finance
new industries was only possible by additional
super-profits from genocide.

"Ernest Mandel shows how without such super-
profits, Europe would have not had the capital to
industrialize:

"*a) E.J. Hamilton estimates in 500 million gold pesos
the value of the gold and silver that the Spanish took
to Europe between 1503 and 1660.*

"*b) Colenbrander calculates 600 million gold florins
for the treasure that the Dutch East India Company
took out of Indonesia between 1650 and 1780.*

"*c) Father Rinchon estimates as almost 500 million gold florins the profit on only the slave trade
of French capital during the 18th century, without
counting the profits obtained from the work of the
slaves in the plantations of the West Indies, which
was several times this amount.*

"*d) According to H. Wiseman and the Cambridge
History of the British Empire, it is considered that
the earnings obtained with the work of the slaves in
the British West Indies were at least some 200 to 300
million gold pounds.*

"*e) Finally, in the pillage of India in the period of
1750 to 1800 only, the ruling class in Great Britain
obtained between 100 and 150 million gold pounds.
If these sums are added up, we get more than 1,000
million gold pounds, that is, more than the value of*

all the capital invested in all of the steam-operated industry of Europe around the year 1800.'

"And Mandel does not even include the great profits from the Afrikan slave trade by the British, the u.s. settlers, the Dutch and the Portuguese.

"The cost in human lives is beyond comprehension, particularly when we want to pretend that it isn't happening (I never knew anything about the gas chambers. How could we know what was happening to the Jews?). Christopher Columbus led the first European invasion that occupied Hispaniola, the island containing both Haiti and the Dominican Republic. By his fourth trans-Atlantic voyage in 1502, he discovered that the once-large indigenous 'Indian' population was being exterminated:

> *"'Columbus was shocked by the change since his last sight of the island, and he was right in saying that the fortunes of Espanola [Hispaniola] depended on the natives. Las Casas was of the opinion that between 1494 and 1508 more than three million souls had perished on the island—slain in war, sent to Castile as slaves, or had been consumed in the mines and other labors. 'Who of those born in future centuries will believe this? I myself who am writing this and saw it and know most about it can hardly believe such as possible...'*

"Columbus was stunned at the magnitude of the genocide he had witnessed, which he thought almost beyond belief. Yet, what he saw was only a warm-up. In Mexico within one century the Spanish occupation had depopulated the land, reduced the indigenous population from 25 million to one and a half million. And had burned the great library, killed the priest-scientists, and deprived the de-urbanized slave survivors of most of their culture.

"The true costs of industrializing Europe and the u.s.a., the cost of powering up Western consumer society, genocide on a world scale. Hundreds of millions of persons were consumed, whole societies burned up in the process.

"The patriarchy has long conditioned us on pain of prison or death to look the other way unthinkingly, to never see the genocide. Without breaking this lock, without confronting genocide, we can never know who we are and what we must become...

"What produces a system that bases its daily life on doing genocide? The answer is, a commodity civilization that formed itself through centuries of repressing and terrorizing its own 'internal colony' of women, killing millions of us. How could sane Afrikans or Indians guess what this strange euro-capitalism would ultimately do? To white men, who were 'made' by a social process in which they shared in the torturing and killing of their mothers, wives, sisters and daughters, doing genocide to other peoples was no big deal at all. Just another day at the office.

"Genocide against women cannot be separated from euro-capitalism, for it is both the father and the

son of genocide against the colonized nations and
peoples of the Third World. It is what led up to
euro-colonialism, and what is the transformed and
continuing wave of that genocide."[18]

There is nothing natural about nations formed out of such
a genocidal economic process. Not too much that's voluntary, either. We want to detour for a moment, to bring into
definition the basic terms we all use. The human race developed & evolved through different types of political units, of
which modern nations are but one. A **tribe** is a community
of people with a common historical origin, usually blood-
related, who recognize a single political leadership. Contrary
to capitalist stereotypes, tribal government was often a
highly-developed system aimed at consensus and dispersed
political power. Both "democratic" capitalism and patriarchal socialism are much more authoritarian than most tribal
societies were.

An **empire** is a State that encompasses a number of different peoples and territories under one sovereign authority. Empires first grew out of tribal expansionism, and most
of those "great" civilizations in history were empires, for
obvious reasons (their ability to concentrate slave labor,
economic resources, and to support large armies). The
Ethiopian empire (Ethiopia was an empire, not a nation),
which fell only in our lifetimes, had an unbroken history of
rule going back before biblical times. Empires existed long
before modern nations did. This escaped many of us, since
we assumed that anything large must be a nation. On the
contrary, an empire like Rome's was almost on a world scale,
but as a State Rome was just one city-state of citizens in the
middle of Italy. 20th century industrial empires are mostly

empire = imperial

capitalist nations that acquired colonies.

There are many *different* types of nations out there in the world. Your prototypical capitalist nation in europe grew out of tribal conquest of other peoples into feudal kingdoms or empires. The size, shape and rules of these feudal realms changed drastically according to splits in the royal families, wars, marriages (i.e. mergers and alliances) to other ruling families, even changes of noble whim. A feudal domain was a personal or clan holding, not yet a nation.

Even the people changed. England in the days of the Plantagenet kings and their knights in armor included one-third of what is now France. Of course, the Anglo-Saxon English were themselves tribal invaders from Scandinavia & France. England's indigenous had long before retreated to remote Wales and Scotland. France itself got its name from the conquering Franks, a Germanic tribe that had come originally in the 6th century b.c. from Central Asia, and that had unified France (and much of europe) in the 9th century. Got that? *heh*

it all gets inter-mixed

So the English are really the Welsh. Some stray Scandinavian and French became the English. While the French were made by and named after some tribe of Asians who now call themselves Germans. What's a poor peasant dyke to make of all that?

With the rise of mercantile or pre-industrial capitalism, embryonic capitalist classes needed a more developed political framework: A State that reflected the territorial size & population they needed as their natural resources; with a centralized bureaucracy to ensure uniformity of economic conditions, laws, taxes, and shipping tariffs throughout the land, as well as armies & navies for colonial conquests. The rise of the Nation-State out of the patchwork quilt of feudal

NATURAL

domains and empires was the long, slow gestation period of euro-capitalism.

A nation has been defined as a stable, historically developed community of people living in a definite territory, who share a common language, culture, and self-sufficient economy. Sounds nice, doesn't it? Nation-building men, from Joe Stalin (who ordered that definition read around the world) on have pushed such idealized definitions because it makes their own nations (or empires) seem a natural community, just and inevitable.

Few nations in the world even resemble that rosy description, with the possible exception of some of the original native nations of the Western Hemisphere. But we haven't thought about it, because we've been indoctrinated since childhood into thinking of nations as natural communities. Since modern nations are supposedly sovereign *political* units governing definite territories, most of which were formed by euro-capitalism, how could they be anything but artificial, imposed, rearrangeable like the furniture? And isn't that what's exploding in world politics right this instant?

The general rule of nations is that they're created to meet the needs of one capitalist class or another. This certainly applies to most Third World nations, which were given shape as colonies or neo-colonies. Iraq & Kuwait gravitated into war because they were formed by the British colonial office as incomplete polar opposites. No Arabs had any say in the Iraq-Kuwait-Saudi borders, which history says were set one night in November, 1922, by British envoy Sir Percy Cox.

The plan was simple: Iraq would be made as a nation out of three ethnic-religious differing Turkish provinces, with much population but no natural seaport and only some oil.

makes it seem preconceived...

Most of the oil reserves and seacoast would go to Kuwait, a tribal nation (only members of the servant tribe which worked for the British are actual citizens. All other Arab clans from Kuwait are stateless subjects) with no real population. "An oil field with a flag." These incomplete, artificial nations could be easily manipulated, the West saw. Former British u.n. ambassador Sir Anthony Parsons admitted: "We, the British, cobbled Iraq together. It was always an artificial state. It had nothing to do with the people who lived there."[19]

euro-capitalism has always encouraged Arab or islamic fundamentalism in a covert way, even when it has an anti-u.s. edge to it, because the fight by elites to make their artificial nations rise has led to men's self-destruction. Like Iran and Iraq, two supposedly anti-imperialist and anti-u.s. islamic nations, spending eight years at war, killing a million of their own people. How holy.

There's every kind of strange male nation you can think of out there. Not only tribal nations, but "racial" nations like Germany and Japan (where citizenship is genetic), and religious nations like Saudi Arabia, Israel and Poland (where the nation is said to be a religious community). Fuhrer Lech Walesa, the u.s.-sponsored david duke of Poland, says in speeches that even Jews whose families have lived in Poland a thousand years cannot be true members of his "Polish nation," but are in a separate "Jewish nation" (his phrases). And more still.

Capitalism even has one-use, disposable nations like Panama. Which has so little reality that its official currency is the u.s. dollar and its former president is doing life in a u.s. prison. Again, this is a nation fully accepted as legitimate by both left and right, in the u.n. and all. Panama never existed as a nation before Wall St. needed a small dummy nation to put its Panama Canal (and accompanying u.s. Army base) into. That area was part of Colombia, but Colombia's local elite was being stubborn, wanting to get cut in on the profits of the Canal. So in 1903 u.s. president Theodore Roosevelt's administration sent in the marines, hired a few local big-shots to be a "Panamanian" government, and "recognized" their dummy nation of Panama.

Panama has no purpose, economy, or culture—*as a nation*—other than serving u.s. interests. It was born with a neo-colonial addiction. The Panamanian upper class (including its u.s.-installed president) are known to the peo-ple as "rabi blancos" (white tails) because they remain purely & proudly european. Most of the people, like those poor slum-dwellers killed by that u.s. midnight surprise bombing during the 1989 invasion, are, however, distinctly Afrikan. Now that it's less useful, with the Latin regional banking center moved from Panama City to Miami & the Canal less strategic, the u.s. is just letting Panama collapse as a dispos-able nation, intervening only enough to make sure nothing too democratic is happening.

No, there's nothing natural or sacred or necessarily fixed about nations. We don't have to approach the subject with any awe. And we sure don't have to accept as binding the nation we are forced into. The reverse side of that is *some-body* is going to consciously make new nations and discon-nect old ones. If we don't take that shot then it just means somebody else will, someone's still going to pull the trigger of history. If the capitalist class can create nations of the most widely varying types, sizes & shapes, including new types never seen before, to carry out its mission, then so can the oppressed in the course of the struggle.

CHAPTER FOUR:

IMPERIALISM AND THE ANTI-COLONIAL REVOLUTION

Colonialism reached its logical conclusion in imperialism, the monopoly stage of capitalism that first began in the 1890s. It was imperialism itself, out of its own internal contradictions, that gave rise to its great opposite, the anti-colonial revolutions of <u>1945–1975</u>. From that dialectical unity came neo-colonialism.   *civil rights mvmt*

For over four centuries, the european colonial system had expanded, attacked, occupied until it monopolized the entire human race within it.

Even the smallest white nations could have colonial empires if they wished. Tiny Belgium, which for most of its history was only a dukedom, a province, or a colony itself of Austria or Holland until it first became a nation in 1830, colonized Zaire in central Afrika along the Congo river. That one colony with its large outpouring of gold, silver, copper, aluminum, petroleum, coal, cobalt, manganese, diamonds, coffee, cotton and other natural wealth, was larger and a dozen times more valuable than Belgium itself. Backward, unindustrialized little Portugal, the poorest country in western europe, could still own four colonies in Afrika and its island colony of Macau in China. So when it came to the major powers, these empires were vast. Great Britain owned one quarter of the earth and compared itself proudly to Rome. France, a country the size of Texas, occupied Indo-China (Vietnam, Laos, Cambodia), many islands in the South Pacific, Algeria, Tunisia and Morocco in North Afrika, and perhaps one-fifth of all Black Afrika.

By the Berlin Conference of 1894, in which the european powers divided up Afrika and apportioned it out between them, essentially the entire globe was owned by one socio-economic system. Imperialism had claimed every person, every piece of earth, every tree and every stalk of grain in the world.

Imperialism as a stage is characterized by monopoly capitalism, which carried the tendency within capitalism towards economic concentration to new heights. In each capitalist nation, industries became dominated by giant corporate monopolies under the coordinating rule of finance capital. In 1901 the J.P. Morgan banking house merged what had been the industry-leading Carnegie Steel and other steel companies into one monopolistic entity, named U.S. Steel. The same happened in u.s. automobile production, where the 108 firms that existed as late as 1929 were merged and winnowed to make only 44 in 1934 and effectively the big three a few years later (with their market protected by a 45% u.s. import tax on autos). Monopoly was the rule in colonial markets as well. There was no new geography for capitalist nations to conquer, no frontier to expand into, since all were held or dominated by one capitalist nation or another.

Up to 1945 the history of western imperialism was a pattern of evergrowing crisis. Vast industrial production in the metropolis only feeding a cycle of larger and larger, see-sawing swings of economic boom and depression. The intensifying capitalistic rivalry for markets and colonial raw materials was only resolved by war, since national monopolies prevented any real marketplace competition. In his 1916 study of imperialism, the Russian revolutionary Lenin concluded that this seemingly inevitable cycle of capitalist wars and crisis made imperialism the final and even "decaying" stage of capitalism. That was a widely-shared judgment.

Economic rivalry on a national basis ran the white man straight into two world wars, where the have-not powers led by Germany (without enough colonies to push their way to the top) felt compelled to make war on Britain, France and the u.s.a., who already held most of the colonial world. By the close of World War II in 1945, this imperialist "progress" had led to the ruin of many capitalist classes, the devastation of europe itself, over 60 million deaths worldwide in the seven years of war, and the rise of a "socialist camp" over one-third of the world. It is doubtful that western capitalism could have survived another round of that.

It didn't matter, since a new force changed the equations of world power, the oppressed themselves. Imperialism, in so violently welding together the world, had exposed people to new ways, new sciences, new social reorganization. It had, in short, given a political education to the oppressed and colonized. Anti-colonial movements of a new type started and soon gained mass followings. In country after country, uprisings and guerrilla wars broke out. A young Black minister in Montgomery, Alabama spoke for the world majority: "We have a determination to be free in this day and age. This is an idea whose time has come."

World War II was itself a catalyst, a great accelerator

WWII was a catalyst

of power changing hands. Colonial rule tottered. In Hong Kong, in Burma and Singapore, in the Philippines and North Afrika, native crowds watched as "their" white soldiers, disarmed and cast down, were marched through the streets by their captors. The mystique of white-ism was punctured. Locked in a life and death total war; the imperialist combatants drew their colonial subjects into the world war. As colonial troops, military porters and laborers, new industrial workers. Tens of thousands of Afrikan men were recruited from different Afrikan colonies to fight in Burma. Many more Asians and Indians were given rifles and told to defend their British masters from the advancing imperial Japanese army.

Contradictions were aching, at the breaking point. There were armed mutinies among the British Indian regiments in Burma and the Greek divisions with the allies in North Afrika. Black sociologist St. Clair Drake tells of how one group of black G.I.'s in the south pacific stepped away from their anti-aircraft guns to watch Japanese zeroes and u.s. marine fighters mix it up in an aerial dogfight—loudly cheering on the Japanese pilots: "*Go get that white boy!*" Then, as a Japanese plane neared, jump back to duty and start throwing flak up at it. There was a major spontaneous uprising in Harlem in 1943, and in the Detroit race riot that same year thousands of whites and blacks fought it out in a chaotic free-for-all (34 killed and hundreds wounded). In the great Black novel of World War II, Killens' *And Then We Heard The Thunder*, his story concludes with thousands of New Afrikan servicemen on leave in an Australian city defending themselves with rifles in a spreading firefight against the white G.I.'s and their u.s. army as the city burns in race war.

Imperialism found that it could not contain the new revo-lutions. In Algeria, the French army and white settlers killed one million Algerians, one tenth of the population, during the 1954–1961 revolution and still could not find victory. In Vietnam, the French colonial army again killed one million Vietnamese and by 1954 had been defeated. Followed by the Amerikans, who fought the longest war in u.s. history, killed hundreds of thousands of Vietnamese and lost as well.

Thirty years of continuous fighting in Vietnam, from 1945 to 1975, ended in suburban white flight. In the Delta, in Detroit, in Birmingham, anti-colonialism was an idea whose time had come.

A people, after all, who can boycott the entire city bus system, who set up systems of armed self-defense, are a peo-ple who can potentially take the power in their own hands.

1945 marks the beginning of change to a neo-colonial world order. Exhausted and bled by war, the other imperi-alist nations gradually let the u.s. empire introduce a new system that emphasized imperialist unity over rivalry. Wars between nations of white men over colonial markets and resources was replaced by NATO, by the U.N. and the World Bank, by the International Monetary Fund, the Group of Seven, the Common Market and the Trilateral Commission. **The key to unity, the u.s. ruling class understood, was decolonization.** Only by sharing former colonies and open-ing national markets to corporations from different nations, could imperialism forestall the savage national economic wars that were inevitably resolved on the battlefield. That decolonization opened up europe's Afrikan and Asian colo-nies to u.s. economic penetration was an added blessing in Wall St.'s plans. That this would someday mean giving up an increasing wedge of their u.s. home markets and real estate

to British, Japanese and German corporations was something that didn't occur to them in their yankee arrogance.

A quick way to get an overview of the change so far is a
comparison table:

IMPERIALISM IN THE COLONIAL ERA	NEO-COLONIALISM
National Corporation	Multinational corporations and joint ventures
As many colonies as possible	Decolonization into neo-colonies
Unrestricted trade wars and national monopolies	Managed world trade and lowering of trade barriers
National ruling class and national class structure	Growing integration of world into one class structure
Industry restricted to metropolis Third World restricted to producing raw materials	Spread of Industry around the world. Third World rapidly developing but in a "pathological" way as distorted expressions of metropolis
European settler-colonialism promoted to serve as loyal strongholds of euro-capitalism: i.e. u.s.a., Canada, Australia, Kenya, Argentina, South Afrika, Israel, Algeria, "Rhodesia," etc. *Settlers becoming new class.*	With decolonization and integration of native petty-bourgeoisie into Western capitalism, white settlers anachronistically and slowly being abandoned as French Algeria, "Rhodesia" and settler Kenya already have been. *De-settlerisation.*

IMPERIALISM IN THE COLONIAL ERA

u.s. defined as white male nation. All other cultures defined as alien, marginal—or criminal.

Women colonized everywhere european capitalism ruled.

Black Nation was white amerikkka's most valuable economic asset, (held as colony for 400 years)

Rule of finance capital Economic crisis resolved by periodic bloodletting, cycles of boom and depression.

NEO-COLONIALISM

u.s. redefined as "multicultural," with everyone having a unique minority identity besides being "American"—even white men.

Trend of women in metropolis being neocolonized (legal equality) while neo-colonial men in most of the world urged to improve their lot by stepping up the colonization of "their" women. *Violence against women up worldwide.*

Black Nation a liability, too dangerous. Being rapidly decolonized by adopting some middle class into amerikkka and genocide for the rest (replaced economically by new Third World population transfer).

Rule of finance capital Managed trade and competition not able to halt gradual slide into world economic crisis. Unclear resolution.

A transformation of such magnitude did not go unnoticed by revolutionaries, although there was a strong tendency to interpret the neo-colonial changes as mere trickery, as cosmetic changes. We greatly underestimated the massive class changes about to happen. We knew there would be a few Toms and Tomasinas, some bribed or sell-outs, but we never thought imperialism would bring millions and tens of millions of Third World people into its middle class structures world wide.

Anti-colonial revolutionaries were also too accustomed to dealing with neo-colonialism as a part of the colonial system (just as today there are still many colonial situations remaining within the larger neo-colonial context). Folks didn't see how it was becoming the dominant reality itself—or how qualitatively different that reality would be.

There were always situations in the colonial era when euro-capitalism was unable to annex a people as an outright colony (usually during a capitalist transfer of power), and therefore they were allowed to become an independent nation but under indirect control of one power or another. The Latin Amerikan nations, which were once colonies of Spain and Portugal, are the classic case. When the local settler bourgeois, led by the nation-maker Simon Bolivar, decided in the early 1800s to be the bosses over the Indian slaves and serfs themselves, England and the young u.s.a. gave them arms and other aid to revolt against Spain. It was simple capitalist rivalry.* In their cradle these "Latin" nations

---

* In the colonial era, it was the rule for euro-capitalist nations to try and weaken each other by supporting dissident forces in each others colonies. Which is why monarchist France sent its ships and soldiers to aid the slavemaster-general George Washington, in his "democratic" revolt against the British empire. The kingdom of Dahomey was able

were neo-colonies of first the British empire and then the u.s. empire. One modern advantage that u.s. imperialism had in the 20th century was that it was committed to expansion overseas primarily through neo-colonies.

By the 1960s it had become clear that imperialism, on the defensive before the anti-colonial uprisings, was committing itself to neo-colonialism. More than anyone else, it was the political leaders of the Afrikan revolution—in particular Frantz Fanon of the French colonies of Martinique and Algeria, Kwame Nkrumah of the British colony of Ghana, and Amilcar Cabral of the Portuguese colonies of Guinea-Bissau and the Cape Verde Islands—who began in their own ways to confront this new development.

Kwame Nkrumah, called Osaoyefo ("Liberator") for leading the first national movement to gain independence in black Afrika, wrote a study of neo-colonialism in 1965: *Neo-Colonialism: The Last Stage of Capitalism*. Nkrumah later recalled in exile that the u.s. government "reacted sharply."[20] An official protest by G. Mennen Williams, u.s.

---

to stay independent of French colonialism until virtually the end of the 19th century, when the rest of West Afrika had fallen, not only because of its large military (whose heart was an elite corp of 5,000 amazons) but because wily King Behanzin had obtained modern rifles, some cannons, and even military specialists from France's rival, Germany.

After having defeated the French several times, Dahomey was only conquered in 1892 when France sent its Afrikan Senegalese battalions, expert at rifle and machine gun, led by its greatest commander, the black general Alfred Dodds. Even the courage of Dahomey's amazon warriors, who fought their way to the black French ranks against machine gun fire, could not prevail against "the discipline and the marksmanship of the Senegalese sharpshooters." Then, as now, only Afrikan men could conquer Afrikans for euro-capitalism. (See: J.A. Rogers. *World's Great Men of Color*. N.Y. 1979. pp. 329–335).

assist. secretary of state for Afrikan affairs, ended omi-
nously: "The government of the United States actually
therefore holds the government of Ghana fully responsible
for whatever consequences the book's publication may have."
Years later Nkrumah said: "It is very significant that of all
my books, *Neo-colonialism* is the only one which caused a
government to register a formal protest." And perhaps more
than a mere protest. In that he warned:

> "The neo-colonialism of today represents imperial-
> ism in its final and perhaps its most dangerous
> state. In the past it was possible to convert a coun-
> try upon which a neo-colonial regime had been
> imposed—Egypt in the 19th century is an exam-
> ple—into a colonial territory. Today this process is
> no longer feasible. Old-fashioned colonialism is by
> no means entirely abolished. It still constitutes an
> Afrikan problem, but it is everywhere on the retreat.
> Once a territory has become nominally indepen-
> dent it is no longer possible, as it was in the last
> century, to reverse the process. Existing colonies
> may linger on, but no new colonies will be created.
> In place of colonialism as the main instrument of
> imperialism we have today neo-colonialism.
>
> "The essence of neo-colonialism is that the state
> which is subject to it is, in theory, independent
> and has all the outward trappings of international
> sovereignty. In reality its economic system and thus
> its political policy is directed from outside."[21]

This simple definition of neo-colonialism, that of "indirect
rule," is generally accepted now.

A year after these well-intentioned words were written, Nkrumah was overthrown by the state he himself had led.[22] After the military coup of Feb. 24, 1966, while Nkrumah was on route to Beijing for a state visit, there was talk of C.I.A. "dirty tricks." It was true that the local C.I.A. station had worked with the coup plotters (British-trained Afrikan officers), but it was also true that for three days afterwards the streets of Accra were crowded with thousands of celebrating students, market women, Ashanti "tribalists," freed political prisoners and others.

Nkrumah had been the victim of the new ruling class and the new state that he himself had helped build.

We can add a quick story of how colonialism was force-changed over to neo-colonialism.

By then, it was an established fact that under u.s. leadership the imperialist world was changing over to a neo-colonial structure. After Dien Bien Phu in 1954 it became a panic, a landslide of decolonization. Engaged in a losing guerrilla war since 1945 in its Vietnam colony, the French military sought a decisive engagement to turn the tide at its fortress of Dien Bien Phu. It planned to use that isolated base as a lure, to draw in entire regiments and divisions of the communist Vietnamese Liberation Army onto a technological "killing field." While the French appeared to be trapped, their napalm airstrikes and heavy artillery would decimate the supposedly cowardly Vietnamese, who would at last be lured into "stand and fight"—or so the French generals fantasized.

But revolutionary socialism had given the Vietnamese revolution powers of social organization and military science more advanced than the abilities of Western armies. After months of tightening encirclement and attrition, in 1954 the fortress of Dien Bien Phu fell. Thousands of defeated

French officers, Foreign Legionnaires and paratroopers (and one woman nurse) were in Vietnamese loser camps. It was colonialism's best-publicized body-blow since Little Big Horn. The whole colonized world could see what it meant.

In Algeria, the Black psychiatrist from Martinique turned liberation theorist and teacher, Frantz Fanon, saw the rippling effects. While desperately trying to hold on to its valuable Algerian colony (home to one million French settlers holding down nine million Arab and Berber Algerians), France was forced to begin decolonizing elsewhere.

Everywhere, anti-colonial movements were being born to fight them. A French nation hard-pressed to hold Algeria, that was drafting seven hundred thousand unenthusiastic French teenagers, that had recalled older reservists, and that had desperately stripped its NATO forces of entire tank divisions to rush to Algeria, could not even imagine fighting wars in twenty other colonies as well. (Che Guevara's call in the 1960s for "two, three, many Vietnams" was a statement of anti-colonial experience)

"A colonized people is not alone," Fanon wisely wrote. "Since July, 1954, the question which the colonized peoples have asked themselves has been, 'what must be done to bring about another Dien Bien Phu? How can we manage it?' Not a single colonized individual could ever again doubt the possibility of a Dien Bien Phu; the only problem was how ... This is why a veritable panic takes hold of the colonialist governments in turn. Their purpose is to capture the vanguard, to turn the movement of liberation towards the right, and to disarm the people: quick, quick, let's decolonize. Decolonize the Congo before it turns into another Algeria. Vote the constitutional framework for all Afrika ... but for god's sake let's decolonize quick."[23]

Nor was this the only pressure forcing France's stiff neck to bend. A France weak from WWII, still hungry for its colonial past, was being kicked and shoved unceremoniously into the modern neo-colonial era. united states foreign policy as "the leader of the free world" was starting to insist on neo-colonial reforms. Washington wanted to ingratiate itself with the anti-colonial feeling coming to the surface, especially in Afrika where amerikkka itself had no colonies to lose.

In 1956, old and new collided head-on at the Suez Canal, newly nationalized by Egypt's radical president, Gamal Nasser. French and British paratroops, together with Israeli tanks, seized the canal in a surprise overnight attack. Their surface aim was to restore the canal to the old British and French colonial owners, their deeper aim was to do what Bush later tried to do in Iraq, end their "Vietnam syndrome."

In a public spanking of the three governments, the u.s. Eisenhower administration (which was Republican) joined with the u.s.s.r. to back Nasser and demand unconditional withdrawal. Humiliated, the French, British and zionists had to follow Washington's orders and give it up. It was bruising notice for French imperialism of its second-rateness, as well as a measure of how committed u.s. imperialism was to coldly clearing the deck of old colonial situations that had outlived their usefulness.

A u.s. imperialism that was prepared to do that to its own white citizens hardly hesitated to whip the British and French into decolonizing, also. This was the same conservative Republican Eisenhower administration, remember, whose supreme court in 1954 ruled school segregation illegal. An administration that sent the u.s. army's 82nd Airborne to take over Little Rock, Arkansas, and escort Black teenagers into white schools surrounded by bodyguards of bayonet-waving white paratroopers. Imperialism was leaning on its Southern white settlers to get with the new program, to decolonize New Afrika before it was too late.

Fanon understood that the u.s. was leading the way to cutting short the anti-colonial revolution. He thought it a sign of what was to come that Senator John F. Kennedy, the young star of liberal u.s. politics, had openly criticized French efforts to hold on to Algeria. In Black Afrika, Fanon wrote, "The United States had plunged in everywhere, dollars in the vanguard, with Armstrong as her aid and American negro diplomats, scholarships, the emissaries of the Voice of America…"*

It was Amilcar Cabral who best identified in that time the key questions of the change from colonialism to neo-colonialism. Cabral was from the small educated class in the Portuguese Afrikan colonial empire. His schoolteacher father named him after Hamilcar Barca, the great Afrikan general who had led Carthage into war against the Roman empire (*his* son was Hannibal). Cabral became an agronomist and chief of the agricultural survey in Guinea-Bissau, one of the highest-placed Afrikans in the Portuguese colonies. He was also secretly the leader of the clandestine liberation army, PAIGC (which he founded in 1956 with only five others), and from the start of actual warfare in 1963 to his assassination in 1973 led the guerrilla army in its victorious struggle for independence.

---

* Jazz great Louis Armstrong was sent on a "friendship" performance tour of Afrika by the u.s. state dept. at a time when the u.s. was busy assassinating Prime Minister Patrice Lumumba of the Congo. He later resigned when the u.s. failed to protect civil rights activity from violence.

Cabral was perhaps the most extraordinary revolution-ary leader of his generation. Certainly, as a political-military genius he far outpaced persons with larger reputations, such as Shaka Zulu or Napoleon. His real parallels are Moshesh of Basuto or Mao of China. Cabral's uniqueness doesn't fully come through in print because his writings are only a shadow of the concepts he brought alive in practice.

Guinea at the time of the 1969 U.N. survey had a popula-tion of only 530,000. It had no remote mountain ranges for guerrillas to hide in. It was occupied not only by Portuguese settlers but by 35,000 Portuguese soldiers, with NATO air-craft and weaponry. There was one Portuguese soldier for every seven adult Afrikans. A seemingly impossible situa-tion. And yet, under Cabral's innovative leadership, PAIGC destroyed the colonialists. Doing so while keeping to Cabral's standard that Afrikan casualties in winning the war should be *no higher* than in "peacetime" before the war began. That is all another story, but we mention it only to indicate that his theories flowed from an intensely practical class struggle in freeing his people from oppression.

Cabral was notoriously impatient with abstract Western questions about "Marxism" and abstract notions of politics based on 19th century Europe. He saw that under colonial-ism the whole colony became a "nation-class," that revolted against imperialism as an oppressed class. Peoples or tribes were functionally as classes to him, in addition to all the urban classes created solely by capitalism.[24] The communal Balantes became the main force of the liberation struggle, while the Islamic Fula, being the most indigenously capital-istic in their culture, were the most pro-Portuguese. When young Fula women trying to join the guerrillas were being captured and given to men as slaves by the Islamic authorities,

Cabral had to personally lead liberation forces to tell Fula chiefs at a meeting: *"We aren't going to permit that any more."*

To Cabral's insight, the weakness of colonialism was that it united whole populations against it by even denying its own native allies and servants their class ambition. It squashed society into a horizontal structure, a "nation-class." Neo-colonialism, he saw, tried to correct this weakness by giving way to or even pushing some sort of national liberation!

> "This is where we think there is something wrong with the simple interpretation of the national liberation movement as a revolutionary trend. The objective of the imperialist countries was to prevent the enlargement of the socialist camp, to liberate the reactionary forces in our countries which were being stifled by colonialism and to enable these forces to ally themselves with the international bourgeoisie.
>
> "The fundamental objective was to create a bourgeoisie where one did not exist, in order specifically to strengthen the imperialist and the capitalist camp. This rise of the bourgeoisie in the new countries, far from being at all surprising, should be considered absolutely normal, it is something that has to be faced by all those struggling against imperialism."[25]

Cabral was the first to comprehend neo-colonialism as a new stage, with altered class relations on a world scale that changed the political balance. The new post-colonial states, relying on national pride, absorbing of former militants into state employment, and development of native class differ-ence, changed the framework of struggle from a "nationalist" one to one requiring an anti-capitalist solution:

> "In the neocolonial situation, the more or less accen-tuated structuring of the native society as a vertical one and the existence of a political power com-posed of native elements—national State—aggra-vate the contradictions within that society and make difficult, if not impossible, the creation of as broad a united front as in the colonial case. On the one hand, the material effects (mainly the nation-alization of cadres and the rise in native economic initiative, particularly at the commercial level) and the psychological effects (pride in believing oneself ruled by one's fellow-countrymen, exploitation of religious or tribal solidarity between some leaders and a fraction of the mass of the people) serve to demobilize a considerable part of the nationalist forces."[26]

This gets into dense reading, but was prophetic then.

> "But, on the other hand, the necessarily repressive nature of the neocolonial State against the national liberation forces, the aggravation of class contradic-tions, the objective continuance of agents and signs of foreign domination (settlers who retain their privileges, armed forces, racial discrimination), the growing impoverishment of the peasantry and the more or less flagrant influence of external factors contribute towards keeping the flame of national-ism alight. They serve gradually to awaken the

consciousness of broad popular strata and, precisely, on the basis of awareness of neocolonialist frustration, to reunite the majority of the population around the ideal of national liberation.

"In addition, while the native ruling class becomes increasingly 'bourgeois' the development of a class of workers composed of urbanized industrial workers and agricultural proletarians—all exploited by the indirect domination of imperialism—opens renewed prospects for the evolution of national liberation. This class of workers, whatever the degree of development of its political consciousness (beyond a certain minimum that is consciousness of its needs), seems to constitute the true popular vanguard of the national liberation struggle in the neocolonial case.

"Another important distinction to draw between the colonial and neocolonial situations lies in the prospects for struggle. The colonial case (in which the *nation-class fights* the repressive forces of the bourgeoisie of the colonizing country) may lead, ostensibly at least, to a nationalist situation (national revolution): the nation gains its independence and theoretically adopts the economic structure it finds most attractive. The neocolonial case (in which the class of workers and its allies fight simultaneously the imperialist bourgeoisie and the native ruling class) is not resolved by a nationalist solution: it demands the destruction of the capitalist structure implanted in the national soil by imperialism and correctly postulates a socialist solution."

While Cabral is often quoted, he is rarely discussed. The reason is that his ideas and life are uncomfortable, not soothing but too honest and hard-headed. Cabral brushed aside the usual dishonest rhetoric in which new "socialist" or "nationalist" states are said to be ruled by "the people," the "proletariat" or "the peasant masses," whose representatives and leaders are always these nice men (never women) from the petty-bourgeoisie with offices in the capital, a full package, bodyguards and villas.

To Cabral the no. 1 question was which class would run the new society, and he said everyone should be honest and admit that in his country it wasn't going to be the oppressed. He was raising questions—the right questions—that the world is still trying to answer.

> "Our problem is to see who is capable of taking control of the state apparatus when the colonial power is destroyed. In Guinea the peasants cannot read or write, they have almost no relations with the colonial forces during the colonial period except for paying taxes, which is done indirectly. The working class hardly exists as a defined class, it is just an embryo. There is no economically viable bourgeoisie because imperialism prevented it being created.

> "What there is is a stratum of people in the service of imperialism who have learned how to manipulate the apparatus of the state—the African petty bourgeoisie: this is the only stratum capable of controlling or even utilizing the instruments which the colonial state used against our people. So we come to the conclusion that in colonial

conditions it is the petty bourgeoisie which is
the inheritor of state power (though I wish we
could be wrong). The moment national liberation
comes and the petty bourgeoisie takes power we
enter, or rather return to history, and thus the
internal contradictions break out again."[27]

Cabral's only answer was to modestly hope that the moral
development and cultural loyalty of the middle-classes to its
people would protect them:

"To maintain the power that national liberation puts in its hands, the petty bourgeoisie has
only one road: to give free rein to its natural
tendencies to become 'bourgeois', to allow the
development of a bourgeoisie of bureaucrats and
intermediaries in the trading system, to transform itself into a national pseudo-bourgeoisie,
that is to deny the revolution and necessarily
subject itself to imperialist capital. Now this
corresponds to the neocolonial situation, that is
to say, to betrayal of the objectives of national
liberation.

"In order not to betray these objectives, the petty
bourgeoisie has only one road: to strengthen its
revolutionary consciousness, to repudiate the
temptations to become 'bourgeois' and the natural pretensions of its class mentality; to identify
with the classes of workers, not to oppose the
normal development of the process of revolution. This means that in order to play completely
the part that falls to it in the national liberation

struggle, the revolutionary petty bourgeoisie must be capable of committing suicide as a class; to be restored to life in the condition of a revolutionary worker completely identified with the deepest aspirations of the people to which he belongs.

"This alternative—to betray the revolution or to commit suicide as a class—constitutes the dilemma of the petty bourgeoisie in the general framework of the national liberation struggle. The positive solution, in favour of the revolution, depends on what Fidel Castro recently fittingly called development of revolutionary consciousness. This dependence necessarily draws our attention to the capacity of the leaders of the national liberation struggle to remain faithful to the principles and the fundamental cause of this struggle. This shows us, to a certain extent, that if national liberation is essentially a political question, the conditions for its development stamp on it certain characteristics that belong to the sphere of morals."[28]

At this writing, Guinea, for example, is a neo-colonial military dictatorship minus any liberation party at all. The neo-colonial petty bourgeoisie, whether in Managua or Atlanta, in real life returned towards imperialism as fast as possible. Cabral's heritage has been to pose the right questions, looking from the colonial era into the uncertain neo-colonial future. The flow of insights into neo-colonialism has kept on. Well over a decade ago, the most perceptive began pointing to many new developments inside capitalism as substantive.

The brilliant Greek economist Arghiri Emmanuel (who was one of those mutinous Greek soldiers in the Afrikan desert in WW2) said in the 1970s that imperialism was actually more and more at odds with its white settler servants, and was starting to abandon them to their fate in country after country.

THE ANTI-COLONIAL REVOLUTIONS
CAME FROM NEW CLASSES

At the heart of the Anti-colonial Revolution was not a return to the past, to pre-european modes of life, but the political birth of new class forces. From the european-educated intellectuals like Frantz Fanon to working class socialists like the merchant seaman Ho Chi Minh, to those from the lumpen-criminal depths, whose universities were prisons, like George Jackson, Malcolm X and the Algerian urban guerrilla Ali La Pointe. These were persons created by the modern industrial age.

Whether in Algiers, Accra or Saigon, the anti-colonial struggle was also marked by urban uprisings. In particular, in colonial capital after colonial capital there were general strikes led by the native trade unions, who were socialist in almost all cases. (A general strike is a political one, not against a single employer but involving a total shutdown of all economic activities from buses to factories.) That is only saying that a young class, the urban proletariat, a class created by massive euro-capitalist development of mining and trade in the colonial world, was placing its weight upon the scales of the struggle.

In the 1940s and 1950s such general strikes swept Afrika and Asia. In Zimbabwe (then the British settler colony of "Rhodesia"), an Afrikan railroad workers strike in 1948 rapidly grew into a general strike that paralyzed the colony. The former white settler prime minister, Geofrey Huggins, told the frightened settler legislature: "We are witnessing the emergence of a proletariat, and in this country, it happens to be Black."

In Ghana, the first Afrikan colony to be decolonized, Kwame Nkrumah's Convention Peoples Party (CPP) had itself been born out of the "Christianburg riots", a nationwide rebellion that began in Feb. 1948 after a British cop fired on a peaceful Afrikan veterans' demonstration. The uprising was centered in the cities, and was led by the socialist Afrikan trade unions. Workers shut down electric power plants and public transportation, as British stores burned and Arab & european merchants were attacked in the streets. Only by bringing in its loyal Nigerian mercenaries and troops from South Africa was the colonial order restored.

In Kenya, Afrikan socialists in the multiracial trade unions (including Asians and Arab workers as well as Afrikan) began a guerrilla underground which eventually won the support of 90% of the Afrikan population, by the British government's own estimate. This conspiracy became famous as the Mau Mau Rebellion of 1951–1956, and even in defeat cast such a threatening shadow that it led to the decolonization of all British Afrika:

> "...On May 16, 1950 the Afrikan and Asian workers in Nairobi (the colony's capital) began a nine day

general strike, which stopped all economic activity in the city. The 100,000 strikers were protesting
the British repression against their new nationalist
unions (which had openly demanded freedom &
independence). The strike spread to Mombasa and
elsewhere. Using troops and mass arrests the British
finally crushed the political general strike.

"This set-back was not unexpected, and only con-
solidated the resolve of the Afrikan working class
leadership to organize armed struggle for liberation.
While the new underground included Kikuyu from
almost all classes in Nairobi, from unemployed
youth and street criminals to small merchants, it
was primarily led by the workers in two unions,
the transport workers and hotel workers. In June
1951 the young revolutionaries took over the large
Nairobi chapter of the moderate Kenya African
Union (KAU). Within the next year, they would
secretly win over control of the KAU local committees in much of central Kenya, unable to fully
take over KAU national executive because of Jomo
Kenyatta's great prestige.[*]

"In the Summer of 1951 the revolutionaries established their clandestine Central Committee as the
supreme leadership of the rapidly growing network
of underground cells. Small armed teams were
started to provide security and eliminate informers.

---

[*] Jomo Kenyatta was a conservative Afrikan leader, educated in
London, who was the official head of the legal independence movement.
He later became the first pro-Western dictator of neo-colonized Kenya.

The central committee took Jomo Kenyatta's oath-ing campaign, which had been going on with rising response, and raised it to a new level with the 'warrior oath.'

"This new, second oath ceremony secretly pledged one to join the armed struggle as a fighter, and was administered on a surprise basis. Once a Kikuyu was honored by being invited to take the 'warrior's oath,' they had to either do so on the spot or be immediately executed. It was a selective national draft. This, then, was the start of the armed movement that the British called 'Mau Mau,' a nationalist movement initially led by the young Afrikan proletariat."[29]

While women came to play a great role in revolutions like "Mau Mau", these leaders were not women. The new unions and the independence parties themselves were led by men, largely composed of men. Some of the new classes were, in fact, still so small and completely male in composition at first that the early generation "married out." (The euro-capitalist assumption that all classes, like the animals of Noah's ark parading aboard two-by-two, must be equally composed of male & female, is simply ignorant fiction. Many classes in history have been predominantly women or men.) Historic Afrikan leaders of the independence generation like Frantz Fanon of Algeria, Eduardo Mondlane of Mozambique, Amilcar Cabral of Guinea-Bissau, as well as Nkrumah of Ghana, all married non-Afrikan women.

No one thinks of women such as the powerful market women of Ghana as a "new" class, since women are the oldest class of all. In most accounts of anti-colonialism, which zoom in on male leaders and armies, colonized women are a minor note. You know, "faithful supporters" and "good help-ers." Truth is that rebellious women made the anti-colonial revolutions. Without the rising of women there would have been few anti-colonial victories on any continent. *This was the most radical aspect to the Freedom struggle.*

The Anti-colonial Revolution was so radical, dangerous, in fact, to both sides, *because it freed within it fresh class forces that had been held down by colonialism.* Ghana is a good illus-tration of this because there was no protracted liberation war there—or any armed struggle at all. Nor was there a socialist or communist party. It's comparatively easy to see, unscreened, fresh class forces begin to assert themselves—and, in doing so, change the situation overnight. That was the essence of the Afrikan Revolution. We said dangerous to *both* sides.

Ghana, of course, has a special significance. When Martin Luther King Jr. and Coretta Scott King went to Ghana's Independence Day on March 6, 1957, as honored guests of the "the Liberator" Kwame Nkrumah, it was sym-bolic of the unity of the Freedom struggle from here and the first Black Afrikan nation to be decolonized. The Kings had become famous in Afrika because of their role in the 1955 Montgomery, Ala. Bus Boycott, which broke open the Civil Rights movement. (The Kings, we should recall, could nei-ther vote nor hold public office in the Alabama of that time.)

Ghana's leader, Kwame Nkrumah, was one of the world leaders of the anti-war neutralist bloc of Third World nations, and was "burning to set all Africa free." (as one of his Pan-Afrikanist mentors described him in his student days).

Nkrumah's story is well-known in Afrika. He was, as the saying goes, "a legend in his own time." A young man from the small Nzima tribe went from missionary school to scholarship study abroad. For almost a decade he lived in amerikkka, in poverty, as he made his way through college. At times his precarious income depended on being a laborer in a soap factory or a fish peddler in the streets. And when he was homeless in Harlem he slept on the IRT riding back & forth to Brooklyn all night.

After twelve years abroad, he returned to Ghana in 1947—and only two years later was the controversial leader of a new nationalist party with over a million members.

What is now Ghana was then the British Gold Coast Colony, put together by rifle out of the lands of the Ashanti, Ga, Nzima, Ewe, Dagoma, and other once-separate peoples. British imperialism had singled out the Gold Coast to be its model for remote-controlled Afrikan decolonization. For there they had no significant white settler minority whose local supremacy had to be temporarily respected, as was true in South Africa, Rhodesia, and Kenya. The profitable Ghana coffee bean crop had always been grown by Afrikan farmers who sold it to the Brit trading companies.

On returning home, the young lawyer Nkrumah was offered the job of general secretary of the United Gold Coast Convention, the bourgy-nationalist organization of Afrikan businessmen. He accepted, although was soon to break with "the reactionaries, middle class lawyers and merchants" (as he scornfully described the UGCC) then in negotiations with the British government, and start a new party demanding immediate independence. The founding ceremony of that party—the Convention Peoples Party or CPP—on June 12, 1949, in Accra, was the largest assembly in Gold Coast history. 60,000 people attended, and the CPP was the passionate voice of anti-colonialism. How could such an organization arise overnight?

The West Indian radical historian C.L.R. James, once a colleague of the young Nkrumah, tells us that the early CPP and Nkrumah's anti-colonial leadership were built by the Afrikan *women* of Ghana: "It may seem strange to the Western reader that the Party seemed to be able to call a monster meeting at such short notice. The party propaganda vans would tour the city calling the people to the arena. The market women could get out thousands of people at the shortest possible notice, and Nkrumah's often-repeated statement, 'the market-women made the party,' conveys one of the great truths of the revolution."[30]

James explains:

> "There was yet another social feature of Gold Coast life, which was specifically African and was to prove of enormous importance to the revolution. For the great mass of the common people the centre of African life has always been the market. The Ewe week consisted of four days, the day before market day, market day, the day after market day, and stay at home day.

> "The traders for generations have been the women (Nkrumah's mother was a petty trader), and this function has been maintained and developed until today a large proportion of the retail distribution of goods, and the main channel through which the distribution of commodities flows from the big wholesale importers to the private home is the market, in small villages as well as in the big towns such as Accra and Kumasi.

"Thus in Accra there are thousands of women in action in the market, meeting tens of thousands of their fellow citizens every day. European visitors and officials up to 1947 saw in these markets a primitive and quaint survival in the modern towns.

"In reality here was, ready formed, a social organization of immense power, radiating from the centre into every corner and room of the town. Instead of being confined to cooking and washing for their husbands, the market women met every day, dealing with the European and Syrian traders on the one hand and their masses of fellow citizens on the other. The market was a great centre of gossip, of news and of discussion ...

"These women, although to a large extent illiterate, were a dynamic element in the population, active, well-informed, acute, and always at the very centre of events. A number of commentators have found the basis of Ghana's independence in the founding of Achimota College in 1924 and the resulting formation of a generation of well-educated Africans ...

"Here is the myth in its most liberal and cultivated form. In the struggle for independence one market-woman in Accra, and there were fifteen thousand of them, was worth any dozen Achimota graduates. The graduates, the highly educated ones, were either hostile to Nkrumah and his party or stood aside."[31]

That Afrikan women were the hard-core of the Ghana revolution—not as wives to political men nor as anonymous
individuals "to swell a crowd", but precisely as women, as a
class or a people in their own right—is admitted by friend
and foe alike. A conservative Afrikan critic of Nkrumah, in a
venomous biography of the deposed leader, even speculates
that his growing rift with the women who raised him up
made his downfall possible.

> "'From the very beginning,' admits Nkrumah,
> 'women have been the chief field organizers. They
> have travelled through innumerable towns and
> villages in the role of propaganda secretaries,
> and have been responsible for the most part in
> bringing about the solidarity and cohesion of
> the Party.' The women kept him in their houses,
> fed him and looked after him when the police
> were looking for him to arrest him, as when Ako
> Adjei's sister hid him under her bed once during
> a police search. They also paid bail for him when,
> for lack of funds, it seemed certain he would go
> to jail; they kept him from debt in the numerous
> libel cases that were brought against him.
>
> "It was when the women—the market women—
> began to complain bitterly about the unbearable
> conditions of life in the country, and to display
> publicly a hostile attitude towards Nkrumah's
> regime that most Ghanaians knew, perhaps for
> the first time, that Nkrumah had reached the
> end of the political road."[32]

Of all the anti-colonial classes released into political life by the national liberation movements, that of women was the biggest shock not only to capitalism but to men's expectation of how the world should be.

To quote again from *Women & Children In The Armed Struggle*:

> "Rosa Parks is a woman that everyone knows. In one day she made Civil Rights history by 'her act of defiance on the evening of Dec. 1, 1955, her refusal to yield her seat on a segregated Montgomery, Ala. bus when the driver ordered her to do so.' Now schoolchildren all over amerikkka are taught about her.

> "In 1990, she was celebrated at a giant 'black tie and gown' benefit dinner for her foundation. 3,000 affluent people, from congresswomen to university presidents, came to pay tribute. Cicely Tyson was the m.c., while Dionne Warwick and Lou Rawls sang. Cyril Neville of the Neville Brothers performed a song composed in her honor: 'Thank you, Miss Rosa/You are the spark/That started our Freedom movement.'

> "So lofty is her place in history that even the racist *Washington Post* threw uncommon praise upon her:

> > "'But, as the parade of stars and social leaders said loudly and clearly during the celebration last night of Rosa Park's 77th birthday at the Kennedy Center, her defiance was such a powerful catalyst for the civil rights movement that the grand status of matriarch is hers alone.'

"Yet & again, how many women pay tribute to the Black women who really did what Rosa Parks is famous for? Long before Dec. 1, 1955, the New Afrikan community in Montgomery, Ala. had seethed under the public humiliation of being segregated in the back of the bus, having to yield their seats on demand to white passengers. Segregation, which was only an outward form of colonialism, was not merely a seating plan. New Afrikans were attacked and degraded every day on the buses. It was common for the white bus drivers to contemptuously throw transfers on the floor, so that Black passengers had to get down to pick them up, or bypass bus stops with waiting New Afrikans on rainy days because the drivers said they were 'wet and smelly.'

"Black women who didn't act slavish enough or who snuck into 'white' seats were called names like 'Black bitch,' 'heifers,' 'nigger whore' (isn't it a measure of how successful capitalism's genocide program is that many Black men are proud to degrade Black women using the language first invented by the most racist white men?). Those who resisted were beaten up and arrested—or, in one 1952 case involving a drunk man who talked back, taken off the bus by police and executed right on the spot.

"New Afrikan women were pushing the matter to a confrontation. There were more individual cases of spontaneous defiance. In 1953, Mrs. Epsie Worthy refused a bus driver's demand that she pay an additional fare before leaving the bus, and

then had to defend herself when he came at her
with his fists swinging. In the punch up, she more
than held her own, but had to surrender when the
police came. The Women's Political Council, which
had three chapters of one hundred members each
(their size limit so that each group could really
know each other), had started compiling individual
complaints and planning a bus boycott. It was the
Black women of the W.P. C.—school teachers, college employees, church activists, nurses—who later
in 1955 were to issue the actual call for the Bus
Boycott, secretly preparing and anonymously mass
distributing thousands of leaflets to mobilize the
community.

"On March 2, 1955—eight months before Rosa
Parks got arrested—a Montgomery bus driver on
the Dexter Avenue line ordered four Black women
to give up their seats so that whites could sit down.
Two obeyed, but two pretended not to hear him.
He called for the police, who got one Black man to
stand up and give his seat to one of the two hold-
outs. But the last Black woman, who was pregnant,
refused to budge and was arrested. Handcuffed,
resisting, crying & cursing at the police, she was
dragged from the bus.*

---

* "By then, the Black men on the bus had quickly gotten off and split,
lest they be arrested, too. This was a pattern, where the anti-colonial
confrontation expressed itself as New Afrikan women against the white
colonial order. JoAnn Gibson Robinson, the president of the Women's
Political Council and the person who wrote the leaflet that began the
Montgomery Bus Boycott, said in her memoirs:

"The New Afrikan community leadership, including the ministers and the Women's Political Council, quickly began exploring this as a test case to mobilize a concerted attack on public segregation. After much discussion, E. D. Nixon, the patriarch of the Alabama locals of the Sleeping Car Porters Union and Montgomery's main civil rights leader, decided against it. The woman was not respectable enough, he judged. She was 'immature', a high school student, rowdy and defiant, and—worst of all—she was preg without being married. Nixon decided they all had to wait until there was a more respectable defendant.

"In October of that same year, a second New Afrikan woman refused a bus driver's order to give up her seat to a white woman, and was arrested.

"'The number of Negro men walking increased during 1954 and early 1955. They walked to and from work, to town, to movies, to see their girlfriends, because of fear at riding the buses. At no time did a single man ever stand up in defense of the women. Although it hurt to be called 'coward', perhaps they were cowards, except for the very few men who challenged authority and paid the price. For at first hint of conflict, the men left at the nearest exit. They didn't dare to challenge the bus operators, who possessed police powers. The men feared arrest and did not expect to get justice in the courts. They had wives and children and could not afford to lose their jobs or go to jail. If they were on the bus when trouble started, they merely got up and got off. Or they avoided getting on the bus in the first place ...'" (Although this newspaper has no footnotes, this passage must refer to Gibson's first-person account: *The Montgomery Bus Boycott and the Women Who Started It.* (University of Tennessee Press.) Knoxville. 1987. [a somewhat different version of the role of Black women in sparking resistance to the colonial bus system can be found in: Taylor Branch. *Parting the Waters. America in the King Years.* 1954–1963. (Touchstone) N.Y. 1989])

Again, New Afrikan women got ready to launch
a long-awaited struggle. But, again, E. D. Nixon
decided that the sister who resisted wasn't a good
enough woman. That time his objection was that
the young woman was too low-class. Angry and
poor, she lived with her alcoholic father in a shack
outside the city.

"There was dissent at this thinking among New
Afrikan women, especially from the Women's
Political Council. They started saying that the
issue wasn't how 'respectable' a Black woman was,
but putting colonialism itself on trial. Freedom
was the issue, they said, and Nixon and other men
should realize that. Under criticism, unable to
stall any longer, E. D. Nixon finally turned to his
closest supporter in the local N.A.A.C.P. She was
a respectable woman by his standards: employed at
a skilled trade, not too poor, an N.A.A.C.P. officer
and the supervisor for the city's N.A.A.C.P. Youth
Council. Her name was Rosa Parks.

"It takes nothing away from Rosa Parks' courage
and years of dedication to see that she was not the
first, not the catalyst, but was the symbol reluc-
tantly chosen by men for a struggle that other New
Afrikan woman had already started months before.
It was fighting women, who weren't respectable,
who were 'too hot, too Black' for the men of the
Civil Rights movement, who first broke the chains
and opened the way. Not just in Montgomery, but
all over New Afrika. Now unknown, on purpose
not by accident. Why not call them X?

"Because men are saying now that they know who
X is. That in the equations of life 'X' now stands for
the known. When Public Enemy raps about 'X' the
listeners know that's Malcolm. When Spike Lee
wears his black cap with the white 'X', we know he
means Malcolm. On one level that's no problem.
On another level, though, isn't it true that in math-
ematics X always stands for the Unknown? That's
why many thousands of New Afrikans (not just
one person who started life as Malcolm Little and
ended taking the name El-Hajj Malik El-Shabazz)
called themselves X. In place of their true family
names, lost long ago in the slave ships and the auc-
tion block.

"To me, X is still the Unknown. Now, more than
ever, the oppressed are X, the unseen Power who
have yet to truly name themselves and define themselves. And who more so than women? Like in that
movie, *Full Metal Jacket,* where at the surprise conclusion the unseen Vietnamese sniper who's been
systematically picking off most of a Marine platoon,
lost in a burning city during the Tet offensive, is
revealed to be … a young woman. The Marines on
the screen and the real life audience in their seats
were both caught off guard. In the movie, as in life,
amerikkka had no name for her.

"The role might have been based on the legendary
Vietnamese woman sniper who in real life com-
manded a sniper squad that completely terrorized
u.s. Marines from the 26th regiment, on Hill 55 up
in I Corps. This unknown amazon sister, who the

grunts naturally called 'Apache woman', so demoralized them that men were dodging going out on patrol. Of course, Marine intelligence officers swore that any woman who could keep killing them so smoothly had to be emotionally disturbed. One young white lieutenant told the press: 'This woman has some sort of sexual problem concerning men—she hates them.'

"They claim their own snipers finally killed 'Apache woman' in an ambush, but whether it was that amazon or another peasant woman in anonymous black pants and shirt, we don't know. Call her X.

"(We can laugh at Dick, so resentfully confused when an amazon kicks his butt, but don't white women share those same values? i just read a book by the lesbian-feminist editor of *MS.* magazine, saying basically the same things that white Marine lieutenant did: women guerrillas are emotionally messed-up and unwomanly. Even this lesbian editor of *MS.* thinks like her rapist white brothers do. That's why you don't know who you are.)

"Or during the 1968 Tet offensive in Saigon, when the world watched and held its breath as Vietnamese commandos invaded the heavily-fortified u.s. embassy compound with stunning audacity. They took over the grounds and won five of the seven stories of the embassy building itself, even raising their liberation flag over the embassy roof, before u.s. troop reinforcements took the embassy back in a fierce, floor-by-floor fight. The

Vietnamese fought and died to the last ... woman?
Yes, woman. For the elite commando unit that led
the most important single attack of the offensive
was an all-woman's unit (led by the vice-president
of the Women's Union). Men's government and the
media, always careful about the truth, have care-
fully concealed these sisters who defied them. Call
them X, too.

"It's not about guns, you know. It's about knowing
who you are. In any revolution, in any social crisis,
any struggle for freedom, women suddenly break
out and become incandescent with change. Because,
really, it all began with us and can only end with
us. Human oppression began with the erosion
of the indigenous communal societies and men's
ownership of women and 'his' children that we
reproduced. That was their first captive labor force,
which by sacred male custom even the poorest man
is supposed to be entitled to. Women were the
first subject people categorized by biology, the first
oppressed race. It all leads back to us.

"Which is why in any social upheaval, any cracks
in the patriarchal order, women break out, begin
being 'crazy' and changing themselves. Oppressors
are thrown into confusion when this happens, but
soon recognize it with hatred as the most fundamental challenge to their being.

"Feminism has always played a strong role in the
revolutionary storms of the Third World, but has
always been suppressed in the new societies created

by those same revolutions. This is the most difficult contradiction of our times. One we will re-examine in the course of this essay.

"Rebellious women have so often been the foundation, at the center, of anti-imperialist revolution. This is natural and, in fact, inevitable. For who should be drawn to armed liberation more than the most oppressed? Women's Liberation has always been an armed thing, and involves the overthrow of the three pillars of the existing order: the ruling class, the ruling nations, and the ruling gender. Women's Liberation was the world's first revolutionary trend. It is still today the most radical and dangerous in the eyes of men.

"When we look at the lives of feminist revolutionaries fifty or a hundred years ago, it is noteworthy how fresh, how modern they seem. In some cases they could be young revs of the 21st century. It is the power of Women's Liberation that shines through their lives. Jiu Jin was born in 1875 and was executed by the Chinese government in 1907. She is known as one of the pioneers in the Chinese women's struggle. Jiu Jin made herself into a feminist poet and a woman warrior, one who had taught herself sword fighting and riding.

"The first woman member of Dr. Sun Yat-Sen's historic revolutionary nationalist movement, Jiu Jin wanted a women's army to free China from

the oppressive Manchu dynasty, the white and
Japanese imperialist invaders, and the chains
of patriarchy. She began by illegally leaving the
arranged marriage her well-to-do family had forced
her into. Her story, as related by Elisabeth Croll in
Feminism and Socialism in China,[33] could be a story
of our times:

> "*She founded a revolutionary society among women
> students and applied to become a member of the
> Restoration League, later part of Dr. Sun Yat-Sen's
> 'Revolutionary Alliance.' At first her application was
> refused on 'the grounds of her sex' ... Eventually,
> unable to resist her entreaties they permitted her
> to become the first woman member. She spoke at
> numerous meetings, often wrote articles for the peri-
> odicals published by Chinese students and was said
> to stir her audience with her passionate patriotism
> and her clear analysis of events in China.*

> "*In 1906 she returned to China where she manufac-
> tured explosives and founded a woman's magazine.
> Both projects were short-lived and within a few
> months she had returned to Zhejiang to take up
> an appointment as principal of the Tatung College
> of Physical Culture. Here she founded a branch of
> the Revolutionary League, raised funds, established
> contacts with secret societies and built up a peoples'
> and a separate women's army at her school. In league
> with her cousin she helped to engineer a number of
> sporadic uprisings which prematurely exploded and
> were put down. Her revolutionary enthusiasm and
> strong feminism aroused hostility, and opposition to*

her activities was such that within a year she had been arrested and executed.

"'Jiu Jin through her personal struggle against the restraints surrounding a feminine role became a conscious feminist. In her personal life she often assumed the name "Qinxiong," which means "Compete with men," and one photograph portrays her dressed as a man in Western clothes with quite a jaunty cloth cap. Her poem "Strive for Women Power" reveals her impatience with men's superiority and repression:

"'We women love our freedom,
Raise a cup of wine to our efforts for freedom;
May Heaven bestow equal power on men, women.
We would rise in flight, yes! Drag ourselves up…

"'Former practice was deeply humiliating:
Maidens, young girls were actually mated like cows, mares.New light dawns in time of illustrious culture.
Man's desire to stand alone, supreme, to enslave us
Underlings must be torn up by the roots…'"

"While Jiu Jin became famous after her death among young women in China, and as a feminist poet and a woman warrior continued to inspire many to become revolutionaries, she was more typical than not for feminists. During the 1911 Nationalist revolution there was continual conflict between nationalist men trying to hold their doors shut and thousands of young women fighting their way into the armed struggle, as nurses, spies, ammunition smugglers, assassins, and soldiers. Women made uniforms for themselves and organized into units such as the Zhejiang Women's Army, the National Women's Army, the Women's Murder Squad, and the Amazon Corps of the Dare to Die Soldiers. The last was an assassination force of Dr. Sun Yat-Sen's party, formed to wipe out key counter-revolutionaries in Beijing.

"More than a patriotic struggle was happening. Young Chinese women by the thousands, and then the hundreds of thousands, were building themselves into a cultural revolution. Not a change in male rulers or governments, but the attempted overthrowing of an entire society and its culture. These women themselves began to go through intense changes of the kind we know. As a public sign that they refused to 'bow our heads' to patriarchy, the young rebels cut their hair short and often wore either men's dress, uniforms, or practical garb of their own choosing. This was a sensation. Reactionary men were enraged. While lesbians here get harassed and attacked by men in public for not conforming, in China then for rebellious women to stop posturing in male-prescribed ways, to declare in their appearance that they were out of male control, was a brave stand defying the real threat of lynching or execution. Thousands were killed.

"Women took these risks because taking part in the Revolution and the armed struggle were a personal means of overcoming the patriarchy around them. In 1927 the new Nationalist government established a women's military college in Wauchang

for propagandists who would work with the army
on its Northern Expedition to finish retaking
the country. This was a communist project, actually. Almost all of the new students were teenagers
escaping marriages. As one later put it: 'Where
could she go, a girl under twenty years of age and
without half a piece of cash to bless herself with?'
There was a consciousness of rejecting not only the
old Chinese bondage of forced marriage servitude,
but also the new Western bondage of preoccupa-
tion with 'love' romance with a man as the supposed fulfillment of woman's life. Croll shows this
in the words of one of the students:

> "As soon as we had learned to sing the chorus of the
> Revolutionary song called 'Struggle', every one of us
> liked to hum the chorus:

> "'Train quickly to become the Vanguard of the
> people, To wipe away the old ways, and Down with
> Love,
> "'Accomplish the Socialist Revolution, you great
> women.

> "Every time they sang the phrase 'Down with Love',
> she said, 'we would always shout especially loudly, as
> if we wanted to warn all our friends that during the
> time of our mission we were not going to give any
> thought to love.' ... She said they were ready to sacri-
> fice their lives in order to create a future society which
> could be enjoyed by all members of society. For 'unless
> the old system was completely shattered, womankind
> could never be freed.'"

***

"Few remember today that the word 'communist' was chosen by poor working class rebels in 19th century europe, following the example set by the 'Communards' of the Paris Commune of 1871. This first socialist and anarchist government by the oppressed took over the city of Paris when the capitalist government surrendered to the victorious German invaders. The revolutionary democracy held Paris only briefly, from March through the end of May, 1871, until the French capitalist army from Versailles (the former French royal estate) retook its capital in an orgy of mass rapes and executions.

"What most outraged world capitalist opinion about the Commune was the self-liberation of women. The elder Dumas, a reactionary writer, expressed the spirit of his class: 'We shall say nothing about their females, out of respect for women— whom these resemble once they are dead.' The correspondent for the London Times wrote with disquiet: 'If the French Nation were composed of nothing but women, what a terrible nation it would be.' Capitalism was naked in its fear of these women, who were feminists as well as being from the poorest classes—seamstresses, prostitutes, laborers.

"In her account of the women of the Commune, *The Women Incendiaries*,[34] Edith Thomas tells us of how the French government retook Paris from the people:

"'In spite of bitter local defenses, the Versailles troops advanced little by little. At the corner of the Rue Racine and the Rue Ecole de Medecine, the barricade was held by women. On the Rue du Pot-de-Fer, women were fighting. On the Rue Mouffetard women brought a fleeing sergeant back into the fighting. In the Place du Pantheon, women prepared rifles, while the men fired. The barricade on the Place du Chateau d'Eau exerted a sort of fascination. An English medical student, who had set up an ambulance alongside it, tells us: 'Just at the moment when the National Guards began to retreat, a women's battalion turned up; they came forward on the double and began to fire, crying "Long live the Commune." They were armed with Snider carbines, and shot admirably. They fought like devils…' Fifty-two were killed there. Among them, a girl in her twenties, dressed like a member of the Fusilier Marin, 'rosy and beautiful with her curly black hair,' fought all day long: Marie M., whose first name at least we know among all these dead, anonymous women who will never be counted.

"'The English student goes on:

"""A poor woman was fighting in a cart, and sobbing bitterly … I offered her a glass of wine and a piece of bread. She refused, saying 'For the little time I have left to live, it isn't worth the trouble.' The woman was taken by four soldiers, who undressed her. An officer interrogated her: 'You have killed two of my men.' The woman began to laugh ironically and replied harshly: 'May God punish me for not having *killed more. I had two sons at Issy; they were both killed. And two at Neuilly. My husband died at this barricade—and now do what you want with me.' I did not hear any more; I crawled away, but not soon enough to avoid hearing the command 'Fire,' which told me that everything was over.'"*

"'But repression struck not only the fighting men and women taken with weapon in hand, or those who openly proclaimed themselves responsible for their acts; it struck at random. Every poor woman was suspected… Any expression of grief alongside the common graves in which the Federals were heaped up was proof of complicity. Any weeping woman was an "insurgent female."

"'As for the women who were executed, they were treated somewhat like unfortunate Arabs belonging to insurgent tribes. After they were shot, while they were still in their death throes, they were stripped of some of their clothes, and sometimes the insult went further, as in the Faubourg Montmartre or the Place Vendome, where women were left naked and sullied upon the sidewalks.

"Rebel women were like 'arabs', like 'insurgent tribes' who are outside of european civilization and who resist the colonization of the Master Race.

"'But among all these women who soldiered for the Commune, a place apart must be given Louise

Michel; her great figure dominated them all. She was everywhere at once: soldier, ambulance nurse, orator. She was to be found in the Clubs and on the battlefields, in the Montmartre Vigilance Committee and in the ambulance stations she helped to organize.

"'She also proposed to undertake a strange mission: that of going in person to Versailles to assassinate Thiers, whom she believed to be the most responsible for the situation. Ferre and Rigault, to whom she disclosed this plan, succeeded in dissuading her from it; the murders of Generals Clement Thomas and Lecomte had already aroused public opinion against the Commune.

"'Besides, they added, "you won't be able to get as far as Versailles."

"'Louise Michel wanted to prove to them that this plan, although perhaps absurd, was feasible. She got so dressed up that "I did not recognize myself," reached Versailles without interference, and made her way into the park in which the army was camped; there she propagandized for the March 18th Revolution, and left as tranquilly as she had come. Then she bought newspapers in a large bookstore. Since she did not lack a sense of humor, she enjoyed reading the greatest ill of the blood-thirsty Louise Michel. Finally she came back to Paris, bearing the Versailles newspapers as trophies.

"'But her courage and audacity were not satisfied with these dangerous pranks. She was everywhere—at Neuilly, at Les Mouliineaux, at the Issy fort—with

her rifle in her hand. "Thus I had, as comrades-in-arms, the Enfants Perdus in the Hautes-Bruyeres, the artillerymen at Issy, and at Neuilly, the scouts of Montmarte"—and, especially, the Federals of the 61st Battalion, to which she belonged.

"'An energetic woman fought in the ranks of the 61st Battalion; she has killed several policemen and gen-darmes.' They gave her a Remington rifle instead of her old one. 'For the first time, I have a good weapon.' She has left us several vignettes of that war, at once workmanlike and murderous: 'Now we are fighting. This is battle. There is a rise, where I run ahead cry-ing "To Versailles! to Versailles!" Razoua throws me his saber, to rally the men. We clasp hands on high, under a rain of shells. The sky is on fire.' She opposed the timorous and shamed the hesitant. A panic-stricken Federal wanted to surrender the Clamart station: "Go ahead if you want to," she said, "but I will stay here, and I'll blow up the station if you sur-render it."

"'And she sat herself down with a lighted candle, at the doorway of a room where ammunition was stored.

"'She also gathered up the wounded and bandaged them on the battlefield. As in the early days at Vroncourt, her pity extended even to animals: she went under fire to rescue a cat. But she was also an intellectual who was introspective in the midst of action. One night, when she was on guard duty at the Clamart station, with a former pontifical Zouave who had joined the Commune, we overhear this

strange dialogue. "What effect is the life you lead having upon you?" "Why, the effect of seeing before us a shore that we must reach," replied Louise Michel.'

***

"'UPPITY WOMEN' LOVE ARMED STRUGGLE. Always have, ever since the patriarchy gang took over centuries ago. Across many years and continents, in different languages and cultures, sisters have the recurring dream of the Amazon Army and of women warriors. The image isn't only of soldiers, but of all women who have broken with 'femininity' and set about dealing out blows against the oppressor.

"In Western Germany, revolutionary feminist guerrillas have taken the name of a famous girl-child 'robin-hood' from a children's story book—'Red Zora and Her Gang.' In an interview given to *Emma*, the German women's magazine, a Red Zora sister says:

"'*Red Zora and Her gang—that is the wild street kid who steals from the rich to give to the poor. Until today it seems to be a male privilege to build gangs or to act outside the law. Yet particularly because girls and women are strangled by thousands of personal and political chains this should make us masses of "bandits" fighting for our freedom, our dignity, and our humanity. Law and order are fundamentally against us, even if we have hardly achieved any rights and have to fight for them daily. Radical women's struggles and the law—there is no way they go together!'*

"There is so much confusion about such a simple understanding. Some white feminists agree with the patriarchy that violence by women is morally wrong, since violence is exclusively a male thing. So often protests used to begin with a spokeswoman announcing: 'This action is completely non-violent; we will not use the tools of the patriarchy.' Such views equate Yvonne Wanrow shooting a rapist with B-52s dropping H-bombs, as though resistance by the oppressed was akin to imperialist war crimes. What's really confused is to think: that rifles or arrows (or electricity or penicillin) and their use are the tools of the patriarchy. The real tools of the patriarchy are the masses of men and their women. When you lose sight of that you lose your orientation to the real world.

"More often, women's violence is thought of in a passive way, only as a justified tactic (self-defense) of last resort instead of the first. As something that we only allow ourselves to use after all possible patriarchal solutions have first been exhausted. What we are saying is something beyond that. All over the world women are searching for liberation, for a new way of life, new social relations, a new culture beyond patriarchy. Women's armed struggle is that liberated space we are searching for. More than a pragmatic necessity, women's armed struggle is itself the generator of new culture. This sounds crazy in a culture which has redefined a women's significant moment as when she gets her first credit card or drivers license. For communists armed struggle has always been the midwife in the birth of a new society. The Afrikan communist Amilcar Cabral wrote:

> "'Consider these features inherent in an armed liberation struggle: the practice of democracy, of criticism and self-criticism, the increasing responsibility of populations for the direction of their lives, literacy work, creation of school and health services, training of cadres from peasant and worker backgrounds—and many other achievements. When we consider these features, we see that the armed liberation struggle is not only a product of culture but also a determinant of culture. This is without a doubt for the people the prime recompense for the efforts and sacrifices which war demands.'

"Cabral's point is easy to see when looking back at colonialism in the Third World, but the same point mystifies folks when it's brought home to North Amerika. We tend to think of culture not as the preparing of the meal, not as sharing the meal itself, but as the icing on the cake. Culture is thought of as something vaguely uplifting, spiritual, peaceful— the opposite of armed struggle. Still, like Cabral's people, so much of women's struggles here has been to build or hold onto these same features of a new culture. These manifestations of anti-capitalist culture by women have really been like contested outposts that the advance or retreat of the movement planted or abandoned:

"Political literacy, women's schools and health services, democracy for the oppressed, shared criticism
and self-criticism, women taking over responsibil-
ity for the direction of women's lives, liberated territory. Many things have slipped through our fingers.
Remember when we knew that the only thing we
had in a hostile world was each other? And now
too many think that so long as i have my individual
career and personalized money market fund, then
those things are no longer so important. As though
our effort at women's communalism was only a
poor compensation for not having lots of money. (a
typical patriarchal way of thinking).

"The reverse is more exactly true—it is the first
outposts of a liberated people that are the true
necessity for each of us. The more women try to
have legal women's institutions instead of armed
liberation, the less we have and the weaker we are.
Which then only becomes the further excuse for
more accommodation to the patriarchy, in a downward gutter spiral. Armed liberation *is* extreme.
It is both mother and daughter of a new culture,
which thrives only in a state of illegality and danger.
'Women's life is a conspiracy.' This has been true
throughout modern history."[35]

'A Total Way of Life Has to Change'

WOMEN, From A1

globe's most destitute women—those who populate the villages, farmlands and urban slums of the world's poorest nations—have only recently begun to test their strength. Throughout the developing world, women are demanding new rights and challenging rigid cultural and religious codes that have embedded gender discrimination in every facet of their daily lives.

Their efforts range from winning the right to sell their products in the marketplaces of rural Bangladesh, where religious tradition often forbids women to appear in public places, to attacks on entrenched legal systems that blatantly discriminate against women. They have taken on Muslim leaders who rule the agricultural villages of Bangladesh and Pakistan, abusive landlords who control the lives of farm laborers in India and factory workers who exploit women employees in China and across Asia.

Coming of Age

"There has been steady progress in the last 20 years," said Anita Kelles-Vittanen, chief adviser for the International Labor Organization's women's programs. "Now the movements are coming of age. With time, the status of women will change, but it will come slowly."

While the efforts have improved the lives of thousands of women in developing nations, the movements have touched

India

Nada m[...]
left, and [...]
women, [...]
were am[...]
those wh[...]
marched [...]
liquor o[...]
the villa[...]
Tangad[...]
In the In[...]
state of [...]
Pradesh [...]
alcoholis[...]
among [...]
men ha[...]

ONE HOUR PARKING 9 AM 6PM SUN

TOW AWAY ZONE NO STANDING →

YOUR STANDARD OF LIVING SOMETIMES DEMANDS THE EXPLOITATION OF PEOPLE AND NATURE

CHAPTER FIVE:

THE POLITICAL ECONOMY
OF NEO-COLONIALISM

The philosophy of dialectics reveals that everything develops through the unity of opposites, of what are paradoxes
to simple observation. "It is a paradox that the earth moves
around the sun, and that water consists of two inflammable
gases," one famous scientist wrote. "Scientific truth is always
paradox, if judged by everyday experience of things."[36] To
truly know anything, then, is to embrace paradoxes and to
find beneath the surface the underlying substratum of reality where contradictions interact into unity.

Apply this to imperialism's emerging neo-colonial world
order, made of paradoxes and characterized by both great
vigor and great decadence. The paradox of a high-technology
economy where the biggest world producers of computer
disc drives and of microchips are the Asian nations of Sri
Lanka and Malaysia, respectively. Where the new productive system harnesses computer chip-guided robots, welding and assembling without cease, together with millions of
women, children, and men laboring under conditions remi-
niscent of the slave working class of the roman empire.

Or a multicultural u.s.a. that simultaneously gives rise
to the meteoric careers of a white David Duke and a Black

Gen. Colin Powell alike. Nothing of this can be fully known without investigating the present stage in the development of the means of production—and the towering neo-colonial class structure that has arisen from it.

That there is a new global economy is so obvious that even Harvard professors can talk about it. Political economist Robert B. Reich, in his 1991 best-seller, *The Work of Nations: Preparing Ourselves for the 21st Century*, is urging euro-amerikkkans to wake up to the reality that the u.s.a.— just as other nations—is no longer an economic unit:

> "As almost every factor of production—money, technology, factories, and equipment—moves effortlessly across borders, the very idea of an American economy is becoming meaningless, as are the notions of an American corporation, American capital, American products, and American technology."[37]

Reich's vision strikes a popular note right now because it faces white fears about the decline of their nation with reassuring promises of high-tech future made for the privileged classes: a global suburb where, to use one of Reich's examples, a Cambridge neighbor of his works on Japanese-financed software, computer-coded in Bulgaria, with hardware assembled in Mexico. Someone of the university race, living by happenstance in New England but really a "worker of the world," connected in realtime by fax and computer to workmates in Tokyo, Silicon Valley, and Paris. Industrial labor, Reich concedes, will in the future largely be banished from amerikkka to unseen low-wage continents of helots. It's not that simple.

In the actual world, while capitalist technology, industry and commodities may move without borders, to human beings there are many borders. Neo-colonialism has not abolished the borders between the imperialist oppressor nations and the oppressed nations, that is, between the metropolis and the periphery, but has re-integrated these jagged class contradictions in a new way. Ask the Afrikan women refugees held in border detainment kamps, who are robbed and raped by capitalist Afrikan soldiers with AK-47s and M-16s.

We know that change, which is the only constant in reality, happens by first gradual and quantitative stages and then violently cataclysmic or qualitative stages. In breaking the neo-colonial economy down into major elements, it becomes clear how much neo-colonialism is both a continuation of colonialism and a radical discontinuity from the colonial past.

1. There has been a worldwide explosion of commodity production under neo-colonialism. The colonial period, which tried to limit industrialization to the nations of the metropolis, had become a fetter on production, a confinement on the natural expansion of capitalism. Now, semi-conductor factories, steel mills and auto plants, industrial agriculture based on chemicals and hybrid seeds to mass produce commodity crops, are multiplying across the Third World. Every commodity that can be mass produced is pouring out in an unparalleled abundance. From televisions to t-shirts, from plastic toys to pistols, dinnerware to steel ingots.

The qualitative change in this expansion of commodity production is that the majority of the human race, which as late as a generation ago lived a localized subsistence culture as peasants on the fringes of the commodity system, have now been integrated into the world system of commodity production and consumption. Societies that even during the colonial period ate the grains and vegetables they grew, wove their own textiles, made their own distinctive clothes, cooked in and stored food in pottery that they made, now wear western clothing, eat imported wheat or rice, use mass-produced pots and bowls of metal and plastic. And labor for cash wages to produce things for the metropolis so that they can buy these commodities. In other words, the qualitative expansion of commodity production is proletarianizing the world.

In 1875, just before the final conquest of the entire human race by euro-capitalism, world steel production was roughly 15 million metric tons per year, half of it in the then-dominant United Kingdom (England, Scotland, Wales and Ireland). In 1950, as a then-dominant u.s. empire was guiding the capitalist system towards neo-colonialism, world steel production was at 180 million tons per year, half of it in the u.s. But only three decades later, in 1980, world steel production had almost quadrupled to 780 million tons per year, with production coming from all corners of the globe. Korea, Mexico, the Middle East, Hungary and Brazil, everywhere.

Easily available in almost overabundance, steel has become so cheap that corporations complain that it's harder and harder to wring profits from making it. When U.S. Steel corporation posted year-end losses for 1991, that was a common event in this marginally profitable industry. While steel is important industrially and specialty steelmaking is profitable, basic steel is no longer a major profit-center for capitalism as it was in the colonial period.

As a contrast, the narcotics trade is tremendously profitable every year, come rain or shine. Illegal narcotics is, in fact, much larger and more profitable to the neo-colonial economy than the steel industry.

Catching up with the velocity of this commodity plunges us rapidly beneath the outer surface of the capitalist economy. As worldwise or as cynical as we think we are, there is still a common, naive acceptance of the capitalist economy as unfair but rational for its own selfish ends; as concerned with the prosaic production of everyday things. Oh, we know that the capitalists are exploitative, polluting, rip-off barons, but we accept our everyday surface experience as the reality—like accepting the label for the contents. Yet, the life of the commodity system is absolutely nothing like we think it is. Capitalism is by its fundamental being irrational and wild, still untamed and untamable even by its owners and supposed rulers.

We've been propagandized to mis-think of narcotics as a social problem, not commodity production; as something marginal and illegal, not as both street and Wall St. Governments make a ritual out of promising "war on drugs", but notice that everywhere that capitalism flourishes—from Washington, d.c. to Moscow—dope becomes a mass institution. In fact, only revolutionary societies have ever stopped the dope trade. Malcolm X used to remind his audiences that while amerikkka wanted to keep the Black Nation permanently addicted, the 1949 Chinese Revolution led by Mao Zedong put a quick and total stop to China's former mass opium habit (now coming back since China's rulers are restoring capitalism).

A few conservative economists are saying that governments should admit that the narcotics trade will never be closed down because it is, in one economist's words, "the perfect capitalist business." That is, the narcotics industry has high demand from consumers who can't stop buying, and a commodity that is cheap to produce with a multiple profit markup. Moreover, the narcotics trade is generic not brand name and almost impossible to monopolize. Very open to entrepreneurs and the easiest biz of all for the young and energetic to enter. So how can capitalism stamp out what is only pure, uncut capitalism? How can capitalism stamp out itself? Even if they wanted to, which they don't. Dope is only illegal for the same reason that prostitution is, so that imperialism has a handle to distance itself morally from it—while also having leverage for controlling and regulating it.

u.s. Labor Secretary Robert B. Reich says that "Narcotics is one of America's major industries, right up there with consumer electronics, automobiles and steelmaking."[38] Only about 5,000 people work assembling TVs in the u.s. Compare that to the number making and distributing illegal drugs. The u.s. Treasury says that $125 billion in u.s. currency is "missing"—presumably tied up in the underground drug economy. We know that in the 1980s marijuana production became the leading agricultural crop in terms of dollar value, according to state departments of agriculture, not only in California and Hawaii, but in Kentucky and other states as well.

Cocaine and heroin are even more profitable. They are major export commodities in a number of nations, most notably the Andes mountain region that includes Peru, Bolivia and Colombia. According to news reports on a u.s. house of representatives select subcommittee report, "entire regions of South America have come to depend economically on coca cultivation."[39] This is a commodity that is not marginal but central in the new world order.

"In Bolivia alone, where the export of legal goods is
about $800 million each year, illegal cocaine exports
may exceed that amount. As a result, the drug
industry has become an institutionalized source of
many jobs. It is estimated that 1.5 million people
are employed in Andean production of cocaine,
and as many as 50,000 work in marijuana production in Colombia alone."

More people work in the narcotics industry just in Latin
Amerika than in making steel worldwide. This is the new
neocolonial economics.

Narco-industry is a paradox in that the illegalized underground side of the business is what's most visible, most pub-
licized, while its legal side in the mainstream economy is
what's most hidden.

In the first place, these commodity profits don't stay buried in closets. Drug dealers don't eat them. They're cycled
into the imperialist economy along with all other profits,
pumping up business activity. The N.Y. *Times* writes:

"The broad effect of drug money laundering on
local economies in the United States is being seen
by bank regulators who have discovered unusually
large numbers of cash sales of real estate, automobiles and boats evidently financed with drug money.
In Dade County, Fla., economists have estimated
that as much as 2 to 10 percent of the area's business boom has been driven by drug profits, often
translated in cash.

"'Either there's a lot of tourists not using credit
cards or there's lots of drug money,' said Dexter

Lehtinen, the former United States Attorney in
Miami. Mr. Lehtinen said that in Miami, some
$220 million in cash has been spent on automo-
biles in the last three years, while Jacksonville
and Tampa had about $24 million in cash sales of
cars in the same period. And in parts of southern
Florida as much as 20 percent of the transactions
for real estate are in cash."[40]

This is more than "Miami Vice." Many banks nationwide are
swelling with what the Federal Reserve believes are narcotics profits being laundered. In the first six months of 1989
Federal Reserve banks in New Orleans, Houston, El Paso,
San Antonio, Miami and Los Angeles reported increased
cash surpluses of from 56% to 219%, even during the reces-
sion. "Money has no odor," the roman slave dealers used to
say. These narco-dollars become part of active capital for
business loans, real estate development, home and auto consumer loans.

New Afrikans point out that Black people don't grow
poppies or coca leaves, don't own any airlines or shipping
lines, don't police the Third World like the imperialists do—
so how can this drug epidemic come from them? Although
they're the ones in prison for it. True enough. Let's pick up a
few real life stories to uncover where the narcotics business
does come from.

Take the "Cali Cartel," said by law enforcement authorities to now be the single largest cocaine operation in Latin
Amerika. Cali, Colombia, according to *Americas* magazine,
was just "one of thousands of sleepy pueblos of Hispanic
America, with little to distinguish it from all the rest. Then,
about the time World War II was over, there occurred in

Cali and the surrounding green fields and blue skies of the Cauca Valley something like the spark from a flint that starts a fire. A veritable conflagration of progress has followed..."[41]

What happened was that the Rockefeller Foundation came to start promoting the new industrialized capitalist agriculture there, teaching peasants how to use hybrid seeds, chemical fertilizers and pesticides. Then, with encouragement from the Rockefeller bankers, international investment was brought in to develop the remote region's infrastructure. The World Bank and the Inter-American Development Bank financed a large hydroelectric project, jumping Cali's power supply by twenty times. Other bank loans developed the Cauca River with irrigation canals and dikes to bring another million acres of farmland into production by 1984.

Once an isolated, "sleepy pueblo," Cali and the surrounding area were brought into modern commodity production. Wasn't that a little strange? How was the growing peasant population supposed to earn the hard currency necessary to make this system work? To pay for imported chemical fertilizers and pesticides, pickup trucks and gasoline? There was no domestic market then (or now) in the far-off capital for vegetables from Cali. Were they supposed to carve out airstrips and fly green beans to Florida? It was like a setup for narcotics, the only commodity that would work in that situation.

Anyone who has heard anything about cocaine production knows that it uses large quantities of ether and acetone, to dissolve the active resins out of the leaf cells so that they can be extracted. A coke processing "lab" uses truckloads of these chemicals in 50 gallon drums (sometimes paying $8,000 or $9,000 a drum). Until recently, the only industrial source for these chemicals in Latin Amerika was Brazil. And

for years every time police in Colombia or wherever busted
a cocaine "lab" they would find the site littered with one corporation's 50-gallon drums, with their name stenciled right
on the side: Rhodia S.A., which made 90% of the ether and
acetone in Brazil.

And for fifteen years nobody ever thought to bust the key
processing chemicals at the known source? Give us a break.
Why didn't Ronald or George send in SWAT teams and
informers, like they did for Marion Berry or Stealth fighters
like they did in Libya and Iraq? Maybe seize factory sales
records and arresting the owners who were knowingly making bucks year after year off drug processing. No, that would
have been way too embarrassing, since the guilty company
was the Brazilian subsidiary of the nationalized Rhone-
Poulec chemical corporation of France. The guilty owner
was ... the government of France![42]

Not only do millions of people worldwide work in the
narcotics sector of the capitalist economy, but the infrastructure of this industry is the legal surface world of banking,
arms, real estate, major corporations, foundations, multinational agencies and governments. Neo-colonialism created a
qualitative leap in narcotics production and distribution as
a commodity (they didn't have to push heroin and crack on
the plantation); it has become a global industry closely tied
to imperialism's distorted development of the Third World
and its absorption into commodity culture.

We know that islamic Mujahadin commanders in
Afghanistan have said that their heroin production for
hard-currency sale to the New Afrikan community in the
u.s. is their people's most important economic activity, the
key to necessary commodities from four-wheel drive trucks
to imported grain (in the mid-1980s rebel-held areas of

Afghanistan became the No. 1 supplier of heroin for the u.s. market, a u.s. state department study said).

In Latin Amerika, the drug business is critical right now in christian capitalist development. So critical that even the u.s. House committee and its consultant, Renselaer Lee III of George Washington University, have had to note its positive results from the capitalist point of view:

> "... the report by the House Select Committee notes, the cocaine industry has 'revolutionized expectations and aspirations within Andean societies, for peasants especially.' It added, 'Television sets, video-cassette recorders, stereos and cars have become available.' ... So for the short term at least, the drug industry clearly has some value, both economically and as a temporary relief from political tensions. 'Cocaine has acted as a safety valve for the Andean countries where the economy fails to deliver,' Mr. Lee said."

The narcotics industry, which in the 19th century was primarily the sale of opium to China by British and amerikkkan merchants, has grown a thousand-fold and become qualitatively different under neo-colonialism. Again, exploring as an example this one commodity proves not only that we cannot judge capitalism by what it says about itself, but that to understand the neo-colonial system we have to go beneath the everyday surface into its substratum of commodity relationships.

While on one level the narcotics industry is a better, more profitable method of genocide (imagine an irrational world in which the european Jews vanished because they paid billions of dollars to kill themselves with the nazi's zyklon-b poison gas, fighting each other for the privilege of doing so, and you only begin to grasp our reality), it is in a deeper sense not under control. This neo-colonial commodity, which has super-human strength, is self-destructive to capitalist society in many ways. They spend billions each year trying to keep its social effects in check. But it isn't the dope. It's the system of commodity production itself that is so irrational from a human standpoint. Go deeper into this.

We don't really know for a fact that the Rockefeller social planners, bankers and agronomists deliberately planned for Cali to become a narco-economy. When they established the Rockefeller Institute's Tropical Agriculture Center there it was one of a number of such centers worldwide, designed to revolutionize in one generation the life of the Third World countryside. They called it the Green Revolution (as opposed to the socialist Red revolution), spreading the use of new hybrid strains of rice, wheat, and other crops to double or triple food production for the hungry world majority.

Was the Cali narco-economy only a good attempt which went bad? An exception to an otherwise socially productive reform? No, if anything it's the reverse. The Andean narco-economy has proven to be the *least* harmful, *least* irrational side of the Rockefeller Foundation's neo-colonial transformation of world agriculture. Narcotics is a "good" example, paradoxical as that is to grasp.

Because of the successful Green Revolution, agriculture in the Third World has become a modern commodity business, food production worldwide had soared to levels never seen before in history—and directly because of this, millions of people have died from starvation and malnutrition. The paradox can be defined as the more food, the more deaths from lack of food. Former famine nations like India and Bangladesh now export food. While the public thinks of starvation as a Black Afrika problem, associated with trans-Saharan drought, most casualties are actually in food-*exporting* nations.

Under the headline "WORLD HUNGER FOUND STILL GROWING", a report of a 1987 UNICEF survey outlines the invisible holocaust that has come from the Rockefeller Foundation's Green Revolution:

> "Despite repeated international pledges to eliminate hunger in the world, the number of hungry, under-nourished people now appears to be increasing at a quickening pace, according to new findings by a United Nations agency.

> "Moreover, the increase in hunger is coming at a time when the world is awash with cheap surplus food, disproving the grim Malthusian predictions that rising population levels will eventually overrun the world's ability to feed its inhabitants...

> "'In the last two years, more children have died in India and Pakistan than in all the 46 nations of Africa together,' Unicef said. 'In 1986 more children died in Bangladesh than in Ethiopia, more in Mexico than in the Sudan, more in Indonesia than in all eight drought-stricken countries of the [Afrikan] Sahel'...

> "This month, the Director General of the Food and Agriculture Organization, Edouard Saouma, told his group's governing council that stocks of grains, sugar and butter were all at record levels and likely to increase, and even in the developing world food

production was continuing to grow faster than the
population.

"As a result, countries like India and Indonesia,
which were prone to disastrous famines, now
export food even though increasing numbers of
their people cannot afford enough to eat.

"'Thus the process of polarization in the global food
system is continuing,' Mr. Saouma said."

This contradiction touched the amerikkan consciousness
several years ago, when Chilean grapes bound for u.s. markets were found to have been injected by needle with poison
as a protest. In a day all Chilean fruits & vegetables were
pulled out of supermarkets and destroyed (in many East
Coast supermarkets almost the entire produce section disappeared). Shoppers wondered what extremism would lead
Chileans to poison their food. The *Christian Science Monitor*
did carry an explanation by Prof. James Petras, a Latin
Amerikan scholar at the State University of New York:

"The recent spate of publicity about the poisoning
of Chilean grapes overlooked an underlying issue—
namely, the conditions under which Chilean fruit is
picked and packed. They may help to explain that
incident:

"Chilean fruit laborers work under abominable conditions. They are employed as temporary workers, earn-
ing on an average between $2.85 and $4.00 a day during 12-hour days, for three months a year. The other
nine months they are unemployed. Over 60 percent
of the farm workers are women, who are brought in

overcrowded trucks (up to 100 packed together), and
who sleep on the ground or in make-shift barracks
without bedding, bathrooms, or potable water. Many
female workers are afflicted by horrible rashes and
skin diseases resulting from the prevalent use of
pesticides.

"The other source of labor is child workers as young
as 9 years old. Armed guards ensure that labor
is productive. Any slowdowns due to fatigue are
punished—wage deductions or outright firings are
common...

"The condition of Chile's rural labor force were always
difficult, but they have sharply deteriorated. Until the
1960s, most Chilean farm workers were tenant farmers on large estates. In exchange for labor services
to the landlords, they received a small house, year-
round employment, and a small plot of land to raise
a few chickens and plant some vegetables. During
the 1960s and early 1970s, Christian Democratic
and Socialist governments carried out a land-distri-
butions program that provided the vast majority of
peasants with land, credit, and social services.

"But with the advent of the Pinochet government
in 1973, over 80 per cent of the peasants were dispossessed and the land turned over to agribusiness
supporters of the military regime. Under this system,
the peasants have neither the security of the previous
landlord system, nor the land from the reform period:
the new owners turned them off the land and hired
seasonal laborers."[43]

That symbolic poisoning of grapes headed for amerikkka's suburban kitchens was an act of desperation by those proletarianized and, in many cases, dying from the historic breakthrough in world commodity food production. A glowing story in the *N.Y. Times* titled "Scientific Advances Lead to Era Of Food Surpluses Around World," casually mentions near the story's end:

> **"Still, perhaps 35 million people, most of them children, die from hunger-related illnesses each year, and 700 million other people are malnourished, according to studies by the World Bank and other groups ..."**

Each year 35 million people dying from starvation and malnutrition, while soldiers with automatic weapons make sure they don't interfere with the beans, grapes, melons and rice being taken away. We are witnesses to un-history, to hundreds of millions of deaths not over centuries but just in the last few decades.

Certainly, well over 100 million people have perished so far in this worldwide restructuring of agriculture into the commodity system. What is cocaine, then, compared to wheat or vegetables? The neo-colonial economy has a commodity life that is unknown and invisible to our everyday experience. You can dream a nightmare world so irrational that your local supermarket is secretly stocked each night with products from an auschwitz. Then you wake up, and discover it wasn't a dream.

No oppressed nation is too poor to take part in this great transfer of food into the neo-colonial economy. Every "aid" project by the metropolis only accelerates the transformation of agriculture from growing food directly for the producers to producing abstract commodities for multinational trade. Susan George of the Transnational Institute in Paris criticized French "aid" projects in Afrika:

> "The latest annual report of the French Caisse
> Centrale de Cooperation Economique lists under
> *food* crop projects a 20 million franc operation in
> Upper Volta [now Burkina Fasso] for the irrigated cultivation of green beans. Never mind that
> these vegetables are not eaten by Voltaics but by
> Europeans as an off-season, luxury dish; never
> mind that the peasant cultivators only get about
> 5–7% of the final purchase price—this is supposed
> to be a 'development' project—even a food project.
> This agency has apparently no inkling that 'food'
> and 'cash' crops are not determined by edibility
> or non-edibility, but rather by *who* does the eating!...Given facts established (by the World Bank),
> i.e. that Voltaics eat on *average* only 78% of the
> necessary daily caloric ration; that life expectancy
> is 42 years, etc. a foreign government or a multinational agency has the duty to finance *only* projects
> improving nutritional levels or to abstain."[44]

But, of course, these agencies know very well who does the eating. This Green Revolution is recognized as capitalism's greatest achievement in the early neo-colonial period. For that reason the Rockefeller Institute's Dr. Norman Borlag, "the father of the Green Revolution," was awarded the Nobel Prize. One last note: In 1989, the Rockefeller Foundation announced that after its successes in the Third World it felt morally obliged to turn some attention to the ghetto underclass. Foundation President Peter C. Goldmark said that social planners in amerikkka didn't know about them:

> "They don't just do badly in school; they are out of
> school. Many are not on welfare; they are hustlers.
> Many are responsible for much of the anti-social
> behavior that goes on in our cities."

Goldmark went on to say that the Rockefeller Foundation
will fund new "research" intelligence projects to go into the
ghetto and identify the troublesome underclass: *Who they
are, what they do, how they stay alive...*" So that the solution
can be finalized.

THE KEY COMMODITY IS WOMAN

The most important commodity in the neo-colonial system is
neither the computer chip nor petroleum, but Third World
women. This one fact alone stamps the entire face of the neo-
colonial age. And why should we be surprised? Wasn't, in an
earlier period, the Afrikan slave the key commodity for the
world triumph of euro-capitalism? Because of the Afrikan
slave and the business of trading them and the products of
their labor, trans-Atlantic trade and the basis for european
industrialization were established. Without the commodity
of Afrikan slaves there would have been no u.s.a.

To break it down some: a commodity is defined as anything that possesses both use-value, that is, that has utility
in satisfying human wants and needs whether essential or
fanciful, and that also has exchange-value as a product of

human activity. The oxygen we breathe, while very useful, has no exchange value and is not a commodity. The same oxygen, separated and bottled for a hospital or welding torches, is a commodity.

An economist during the Afrikan slave trade days once wrote : "A Negro is a Negro. He only becomes a slave under certain conditions. A cotton-spinning jenny is a machine for spinning cotton. It becomes capital only in certain relations. Torn from these relationships it is no more capital than gold in itself is *money* or sugar the price of sugar."[45] Understanding a commodity, then, is to locate it in the mosaic of relationships.

In Third World factories making the export commodities that chain their countries to the metropolis, the workers peering through microscopes assembling computer chips or sewing together Calvins and acrylic sweaters are young women. Young Third World women are at the overseas production base of many corporations. This is well known. The key is not that Third World women are super-exploited but that they are themselves a commodity, property. The invisible commodity that, like the Afrikan slavery before them, defines the entire system above them.

Colonialism ultimately fell, as Cabral recognized, because it held down native society into a horizontal "nation-class" united against it; in counter, the dynamic of neo-colonialism is to help native society develop into a vertical class structure with native pro-capitalist forces that are, consciously or unconsciously, aligned towards imperialism. The first and most basic vertical differentiation is for women to become the property of men. As we discussed earlier, this is the genocidal development path that euro-capitalism itself found to build its new nations and emerge out of feudalism.

It is in the nature of wage-labor for workers to sell their working lives, their labor-power, as a commodity alienated from themselves, to capitalism. On the surface, this is what these sisters do as an everyday survival deal—what's assumed to be a poorer version of you or me. There's a qualitative difference. Third World women have been pushed further downward in country after country as part of neo-colonialism's modern development process.

First of all, to bond Third World men into the culture of capitalism by giving them real property of their own, "their" women: for a man to use as a sex-object, servant, beast of burden, unpaid laborer, reproducer of "his" children, even as a source of small cash that a man can expropriate as his own. This is easily understood by anyone who wants to know it. Fresh incidents pop up daily in the capitalist media (the mass rapes and killings of schoolgirls by schoolboys in Kenya one day, the purchase of unwilling girl-children for "wives" by Arab Muslims the next), with the clear intent of showing how lucky women are here to be with "Mr. America."

The paradox of how capitalism produces a trend of equal rights for some women in the metropolis and a trend of increasing lack of rights and degradation for other women in the periphery, is something we should go to the heart of.

This ownership of these women by men, while naked for all to see in its oppression, is still only a strand on the surface weave of capitalism. For imperialism is a jealous patriarch. The outward form of Third World women's ownership by "their" men only facilitates, as it conceals, the overriding and primary ownership of Third World women by imperialism, which has let their junior capitalist partners in the Third World commodify women as instruments of national development. To be used in the most profitably brutal way to earn hard-currency from the metropolis, to be violently used up and discarded at a pace of exploitation so rapid that it is even cheaper than chattel slavery was.

In Bangladesh, for example, young women of the age we usually term children have been placed into semi-slavery in new hard-currency industries no matter what men think about it. A 1988 report from Dhaka, Bangladesh, shows how these young women are provided for international corporations by local government and local capitalist entrepreneurs:

> "Shafia Khatun has made a pioneering journey from rural poverty to a low-paying job in a crowded garment factory, and she may never be able to go home again.

> "Part of a small new industry fueled by American imports, she and 200,000 other women have defied Islamic tradition and planted the seeds of a slow social transformation in this nation.

> "Village elders objected to her leaving home to work in the big city, Miss Khatun said in an interview at her tiny dirt-floored rented room. 'It will be difficult for me to live in my village again ...,' she said.

> "For the same reason, and because she cannot afford the traditional wedding payment, her chances of finding a husband have also been reduced, said Miss Khatun, who at the age of 14 is already eligible for marriage.

> "The labor of women like Miss Khatun is a boon to this nation that has relied on exports of animal hides, jute and tea for most of its foreign earnings.

Planners here now dare to talk, with guarded hope, of industrialization...

"Clothing exports to the United States grew from $45 million in 1984 to more than $300 million last year, making Bangladesh the sixth-largest supplier of apparel to America.

"'This is the cheapest country where you can work,' said Paolo Tacchinardi, a garment manufacturer from Milan.'You can pay the workers, the manager and the shipper, and the shirt is still three times less when it arrives in Italy...'

"Redwan Ahmed, the owner of Saleha Garments Ltd., where Miss Khatun works, said women are essential to his industry. Bred to subservience, he said, they will work for as little as $13 a month and will accept harsh conditions and long hours without complaint..."[46]

A modernization process in which women are "bred to subservience," devalued, conditioned to accept inhuman treatment, and follow male authority, is not so much a prescription for tribalism as it is a social conditioning to be a human commodity in the new multinational economy. Economic planners consciously see the hope for industrialization from women as an export-industry. The controversial Calvin Klein jeans ads, in which women's bodies are presented in soft-core porn, as objects owned by men, is only the cultural expression of the real-life relationship of which those jeans are a product.

The Philippine neo-colonial government—even under figurehead president Cory Aquino—has an official policy of exporting Filipino women as a hard-currency commodity. "They are one of our top ten foreign-exchange earners," more than sugar or mining, said a Filipino expert on the subject. "They're lumped among the best exports that we have. People don't like being lumped with a product, but there you are."[47]

The capitalist program of commodifying Filipino women has succeeded so well that they have become, in much of the world, like a brand-name product. "The Philippines has virtually become a country of maids, cheap domestic labor to clean up after the rest of the world," Labor Secretary Franklin Drilon told the N.Y. Times. The story reported Filipino women have become so familiar as products that "Filipino women traveling abroad, including members of official delegations, say it is often assumed both by local residents and their own countrymen that they are domestics or even prostitutes."[48]

The story continues to say: "The export of labor is a conscious policy begun more than a decade ago to...boost foreign exchange earnings...But along with badly needed dollars, the women have sent home tales of exploitation that include harsh conditions, long hours, underpayment, physical abuse and sexual harassment.

> "In parts of Europe and Asia, particularly Japan, Filipino women are also pre-eminent as entertainers. These women often complain that they are required to have sexual relations with customers as part of their duties.

> "In addition, the Philippines has become a prime source of what are known as 'mail-order brides'...

> "Filipinos sometimes ask themselves how their

women have come to be regarded as a commodity
in the eyes of the world. Organizations involved in
the rights of women and migrant workers say that
poverty and a sense of family obligation are primary reasons.

"Overseas workers or mail order brides are often
selected by their families to support aged parents
and put brothers and sisters through school..."

Prostitution, which is passed off as some fringe lumpen activity (like narcotics), is really a major hard-currency industry
in the periphery. Not "part of their customs" as white men
love to say, but a direct result of the neo-colonial bringing
together of metropolis and periphery. Saigon, we remember and will not forget, had a total population of 400,000 in
1965 when the u.s. troops invaded. Ten years later when the
war ended, Saigon alone held 400,000 Vietnamese women
who had been forced into prostitution. Once a Havana or
a Tijuana would be a "sin city" playground for white men.
Now, whole Third World nations are turned by their capitalist governments into hard-currency playgrounds for
european, amerikkkan and Japanese tourists. What is called
sex tourism.

In South Korea, a land where steel-helmeted security
troops of the corporation, armed with M-16s and heavy
weapons, stand over the workers at the Hyundai steel mill,
a recent estimate by a women's project was that one out of
every six South Korean women between the ages of 15–35
was in the sex industry.[49]

Tourism is Thailand's biggest source of foreign exchange,
with 4 million tourists a year arriving. According to one survey, one third of them say they intend to have sex with a Thai.

Many men come on the infamous sex tourism charter flights arranged by Lufthansa, Japan Airlines, and other airlines, in which the men are bused in groups to a variety of brothels. Bangkok police estimate that there are 500,000 prostitutes in Bangkok alone, with perhaps another 250,000 in the rest of Thailand. (government health officials estimated that 250,000 were HIV positive as of August, 1991)[50]

Thai government leaders, who depend on selling Thai women as a key commodity in their world trade, defend prostitution as better than concubinage or "minor wives" in polygamy. They emphasize how it is supposedly "voluntary", with "only" an estimated 15,000 of the young prostitutes actually being held as slaves (women-children are purchased in the rural North for less than $75). Suvit Yodmani, head of the Thai National Identity Office (and what a strange place that must be) says:

> "In a way, voluntary prostitution has its place, because it helps eliminate the 'minor-wife' phenom-enon. But we must do more to eliminate involuntary prostitution."[51]

Dr. Debhanon Muangman, dean of the School of Public Health at Mahidol University, commented: "There's a law against selling people, but it's not enforced." How can a law against selling commodities be enforced under capitalism?

What all these Third World women have in common is being a unique commodity. They are almost all young, sometimes very young. While the process is most advanced in Asia, where the level of local capitalist development is correspondingly the most advanced in the Third World, it is present in the Caribbean, Latin Amerika, and Afrika. Their existence as a commodity is not a normal relationship, not a normal life. They are exchanged for hard-currency by their own capitalist governments as the very cheapest labor, often paid less than the cost of sustaining & reproducing life. Women who are young and fit, who can be used so cheaply it staggers the imagination, who are made marginal to their societies, disposable after being used up. A. Sivanandan of London's Institute of Race Relations wrote:

> "…For the chip produced in the pleasant environs of 'Silicon Valley' in California has its circuitry assembled in the toxic factories of Asia. Or, as a Conservative Political Center publication puts it: 'While the manufacture of the chips requires expensive equipment in a dust-free, air-conditioned environment little capital is necessary to assemble them profitably into saleable devices. And it is the assembly that creates both the wealth and the jobs.'

> "Initially the industry went to Mexico, but Asia was soon considered cheaper. (Besides, 'Santa Clara was only a telex away.') And even within Asia the moves were to cheaper and cheaper areas: from Hong Kong, Taiwan, South Korea, and Singapore in the 1960s, to Malaysia in 1972, Thailand in 1973, the Philippines and Indonesia in 1974, and soon to Sri Lanka. The manager of a plant in Malaysia explained how profitable these moves had been. 'One worker working one hour produces enough to pay the wages of 10 workers working one shift plus all the costs of materials and transport.'

> "But the moves the industry makes are not just from country to country but from one batch of workers

to another within the country itself. For the nature
of the work—the bonding under a microscope of
tiny hair-thin wires to circuit boards on wafers of
silicon chip half the size of a fingernail—shortens
working life.'After three or four years of peering
through a microscope,' reports Rachel Grossman,
'a worker's vision begins to blur so that she can no
longer meet the production quota.'

"But if the microscope does not get her (Grandma,
where are your glasses? is how electronic workers
over 25 are greeted in Hong Kong), the bonding
chemicals do.* And why 'her'? Because they are
invariably women. For, as a Malaysian brochure
has it, 'The manual dexterity of the oriental female
is famous the world over. Her hands are small and
she works fast with extreme care. Who, therefore,
could be better qualified by nature and inheritance
to contribute to the efficiency of a bench assembly
production line than the oriental girl?'

"To make such intense exploitation palatable,
however, the multinationals offer the women a
global culture—beauty contests, fashion shows,
cosmetic displays, and disco dancing—which in
turn enhances the market for consumer goods and
Western beauty products. Tourism reinforces the
culture and reinforces prostitution (with packaged

---

* "Workers who must dip components in acids and rub them with sol-
vents frequently experience serious bums, dizziness, nausea, sometimes
even losing their fingers in accidents. It will be 10 to 15 years before the
possible carcinogenic effects begin to show up in the women ..."

sex tours for Japanese businessmen), drug selling, child labor. For the woman thrown out of work on the assembly line at an early age, the wage earner for the whole extended family, prostitution is often the only form of livelihood left.

"A global culture, then, to go with a global economy..."[52]

Some economists say we live in a "petroleum economy," shaped by the use of petroleum products. This is obvious. Other social analysts—such as Robert B. Reich—say we are in a "Silicon Age," when this microchip technology is revolutionizing production & communications just as the introduction of steam-engine power did two centuries ago. This is clearly true, also. Computers and tankers full of gasoline loom all the larger in everyone's minds for being so visible in our society. Both of these statements can be true, although seemingly at odds, because they are two strands among an infinity in the surface of economic life.

When James Watt of Scotland invented the modern steam engine in the 18th century, that revolutionized the world economy. Steam power made possible the modern factory, the modern transportation system of railroads and steamships that shrank the globe, and later, the introduction of electricity for household & industry. Yet, the steam-engine was not the most important commodity in the world expansion of capitalism: the Afrikan slave was.

For the extraordinary profits from the Afrikan slave trade paid for the industrializing of Western Europe, for the building of great cities, naval fleets and new capitalist nations in North Amerika—in other words, for the euro-capitalist world empires. The crude and "backward" slave plantation was the unseen foundation beneath the amazing progress of euro-capitalist civilization. Which is why the cultural impact of that commodity relationship still reverberates so strongly in our lives today.

In such a way, the Third World woman is "backward" and largely invisible from the daily life of the metropolis since she isn't selling junk bonds or starting software corporations. We're not saying that as a human experience working in a garment sweatshop for $20 a month is equivalent to being torn out of Afrika and sold on the auction block. That would be silly. *We're discussing the economic role of commodities.* And here there *is* a parallel, because it is these women's designation as a unique commodity that underlies the new world order. Planners in Bangladesh, one of the poorest nations on earth, can hope for industrialization by exchanging this unique commodity for hard currency with u.s. and european corporations. Third World women as a commodity are the key to the vigorous capitalist development taking place in the periphery of neo-colonialism.

Simultaneously, it is the extraordinary profits from them as a commodity that is paying for the brilliant parasitic economy of the metropolis. For example: there is an entire industry, like a fascinating narcotic itself, consuming literally hundreds of millions of dollars promoting & advertising Nike's "Air Jordans." Television stations, sports leagues, posters, magazines, ad agencies, artists and executives and secretaries, managers and stockholders, all take profits and salaries out of this promotion. To say nothing of banks and shopping malls.

Yet & again, none of this does anything tangible for the shoe—it doesn't make so much as one shoelace. How is it possible to pay for all these people and businesses? The

answer is that the top of the line 1992 "Air Jordan" that sells
for $130, Nike itself buys from its Asian contractors for just
$30, including labor, materials and their own local profits.[53]
So a $130 sneaker with pennies of direct labor in it supports
$100 in "welfare" for layers of parasitic businesses in the u.s.a.
Multiply this by billions & billions.

Out of these Third World women's labor and lives is
made the computer chips, the televisions, the VCRs and
other electronic consumer goods, the levis, industrial products, the always in season fruits and vegetables, the donna
karan dresses, the athletic sweatshirts—and so cheaply
they're almost like free for the neo-imperial metropolis. The
kind of profits that the multinational corporations make out
of $15 or $25 a month women haven't been seen since chattel
slavery. This is the commodity that above all others deter-
mines the new culture of the neo-colonial world order.

2. *The global economy of neo-colonialism has been exploded
into shape by historic tendencies within capitalism towards both
the concentration of capital & the domination of finance capital—only carried now to a higher level.* This economy of the
multinational corporations does not so much cross old borders as it increasingly operates on a transnational level above
nations & their governments. Like the sonic booms shaking
houses in the wake of a jet's passing, the operations of the
multinational corporations and their interests leave in their
wake growing crises & destabilization in the economic and
political life of nations below them.

The real map of the emerging world, the lines of neo-
colonial production, labor, and trade, no longer correlate to
the map in our heads of the dinosaur nations of the 20th
century. *This has far-reaching consequences.* This is what the

breakup of the u.s.s.r. foreshadowed. Why even countries we assume are permanent, like Italy and Great Britain, are starting to unravel. And amerikkka, too, of course.

Two groupings before any others have recognized this reality—the transnational capitalist class & the new wave of explorers from the Third World—and are putting themselves into the creation of political-economic entities more fitting to the age. In that sense, the socialist *colonias* or radical squatter communities in Northern Mexico where thousands of workers live and the european Common Market are both forms of this change.

GLOBALIZATION:
NEW STAGE IN CAPITAL CONCENTRATION

The concentration of capital—for the big corporation to swallow the smaller, for the competition of many capitalists to result in the survival of the few—is "genetically" inherent in capitalism. So much so that a european cultural critic foreseeing its future around the time of the u.s. Civil War, could write about:

> "... the action of the immanent laws of capitalistic production itself, by the centralization of capital. One capitalist always kills the many. Hand in hand with this centralization, or this expropriation of many capitalists by few, develop, on an ever-expanding scale, the co-operative form of the labor process, the conscious technical application of

science, the methodical cultivation of the soil, the
transformation of the instruments of labor into
instrument of labor only usable in common ... the
entanglement of all peoples in the net of the world
market, and this, the international character of
the capitalistic regime. Along with the constantly
diminishing number of the magnates of capital,
who usurp and monopolize all advantages of this
process of transformation, grows the mass of misery,
oppression, slavery, degradation, exploitation ..."[54]

Concentration of capital is an underlying evolution, overriding national boundaries, traditions, and cultures of corporations and capitalists. The late Sam Walton, amerikkka's
wealthiest "rags to riches" individual entrepreneur, exhorted
his employees every day to bring even lower prices to the consumer—in the best amerikkkan tradition. Yet, his Wal-Mart
mass discount store chain, in its rise, of necessity crushed,
bankrupted & absorbed the business of many thousands of
family-owned local drugstores & retail outlets.

An article on the trend of the largest electronics corporations to join in even more powerful multinational alliances,
noted:

"Siemens A.G. of Germany and the I.B.M. Corporation in 1991 forged what may become the industry's most dynamic partnership, one likely to reach
across a startling range of chip technologies ... but
just behind them are Texas Instruments Inc. and
Hitachi Ltd. of Japan, which recently announced
that their researchers, fresh from the joint development of a 16 megabit memory chip, were headed

for the 64 megabit generation. Then there is the
Motorola-Toshiba team, the A.T.&T.-NEC pas
de deus and—in what is already proving to be the
most politically explosive alliance—I.B.M. and
Toshiba, which a few months ago began jointly
developing and manufacturing color liquid crystal
display screens for laptop computers ...

"But in the end, what is driving the alliances is not
politics but money. Designing an elaborate new
chip and building the factory to produce it has
become a half-billion dollar enterprise. No one
wants to take that kind of risk alone."[55]

The nationalistic Japanese *keiretsu* corporations, which have
their cultural roots in feudalism and whose male employees
pledge life-long loyalty as though they were samurai taking the colors of an aristocratic clan, now must make basic
alliances to share technology & production with foreign
competitors (even though these Japanese corporations are
already the largest in the world).

What is moving the concentration of capital over national
and continental lines is simple: the need for greater technology, capital, and markets than any one nation possesses.

As the process of concentration bursts out of national borders, the economic table stakes to be a player keep growing.
The old ideal of the self-sufficient capitalist nation is now as
out-moded as the code of bushido. Industries are now more
powerful than nations. If I.B.M., the most dominant corporation both marketwise and technologically that capitalism
has ever seen, confesses that it now needs to join with other
corporations to survive, is it any surprise that the u.s. electronics industry decided to specialize and totally leave VCR

production, for example, to others. Or that Czechoslovakia has sold its entire automobile industry—traditionally, the strongest in eastern europe—to Volkswagon? Just as the entertainment industry in Japan or Italy doesn't even pretend to be competing with Hollywood films, which are big money-makers in everyone's theaters.

Capital, while it still has the flesh habits of its primordial national origins, is learning to think of itself as a transnational being. In the 1950s, world-dominant u.s. corporations began "gate-crashing" other national markets, while "runaway" shops took textiles and other light industrial production to Puerto Rico and other low wage areas. Western europe began, at u.s. prodding, years of startup for the Common Market. The u.s. policy decision to industrialize capitalist Asia was made. By the 1960s, the largest national corporations began assuming multinational dimensions.

In a famous statement, Harold Geneen, chairman & empire-builder of the first multinational—International Telephone & Telegraph Corp. —was quoted as saying that I.T.&T.'s ideal nationality would be to headquarter itself on an island that it owned, becoming its own government and nationality.

In the 1970s, both the Trilateral Commission—the first, informal capitalist world executive—and the european Common Market fully emerged. Few paid attention twenty years ago when David Rockefeller of the Chase Manhattan Bank demanded that national governments must give up their economic powers, their trade laws and protected industries to "lift the siege against the multinational enterprises so that they might be permitted to get on with the unfinished business of developing the world economy."[56]

Twenty years later we find that Motorola, which was then

a much smaller Chicago corporation supplying the domestic market with radios and TVs, is now a world leader in military/police communications and portable telephone systems. Half of its sales are outside the u.s.; 40% of its employees are also. Motorola has a major chip factory in Malaysia (as do Texas Instruments and Hewlett-Packard). Even 25% of its engineering and product design are done abroad. Both a plant in Florida and another plant in Malaysia produce electronic telephone pagers—but the design/engineering center for this division is at Motorola's Malaysian plant, not the one in Florida.

Motorola chairman Robert H. Galvin makes it clear that the corporation claims no bias and wants no bias towards amerikkka in such decisions:

> "We'd try to make a balanced decision that took everyone into consideration, Malaysians and Americans. We need our Far Eastern customers, and we cannot alienate the Malaysians. We must treat our employees all over the world equally."[57]

A common theme in corporate planning now is to place investment, sites, labor, where they make the most sense in terms of the industry—disregarding or trying to disregard nationally where that is. So Texas Instruments, which is amerikkka's leading producer of microchips, has its headquarters and research center for that main division not in Texas but in Tokyo. Just as Nissan styled its new Infinity J30 sedan and other new models at a $100 million design center outside Detroit. Honda, which is a Big Three automaker in the u.s.a. but an also-ran in Japan, has been rumored in Japanese business circles to be considering moving its own headquarters to Los Angeles to become more "American" a corporation. Whether it happens or not isn't the point, it's that even the possibility shows a changed outlook.

FALLOUT FROM GLOBALIZATION

The truth or consequences of this evolutionary march has destabilized many nations—while it has opened upward mobility for the opportunistic classes. One consequence is that the multinational corporations are pulling back from amerikkka (rats know to leave the sinking ship). Gus Tyler, long-time research director for the International Ladies Garment Workers (AFL-CIO), says: "There is a decoupling of the corporation from the country; that is what is developing. The country can be facing economic disaster, and the global corporation can avoid it."[58]

As u.s. corporations increase their employment abroad, they inevitably slim down their payrolls & investment in the u.s.a. Economists and social analysts have been publicly discussing the phenomenon—new to euro-amerikans—of "diminishing opportunities." Reverse generational progress. They warn that coming white generations will have neither the income growth nor the job security that their parents enjoyed. And isn't that a given, now? Assumptions of automatic affluence for college-educated have been shredded like old credit cards. NBC Nightly News reported that the Fortune 500 corporations, which in 1980 employed 16 million in the u.s., now employ only 11 million (and are projected to employ only 8 million by the year 2000). NBC's news anchor then asked a consultant on white-collar employment what middle-class people could do since corporations no longer were loyal in the old sense, even to their managers and professional staff? That consultant clearly caught the wave when she coolly replied: "We are *all* self-employed now."[59]

Corporations, which never treated their colonies or workers as human, are now finding even imperialist national loyalties too constricting. "There is no mindset that puts this country first," says Cyril Sienart, chief financial officer of Colgate-Palmolive.[60] The President of the NCR Corporation (what used to be National Cash Register Co.) remarked in 1989:

> "I was asked the other day about United States competitiveness and I replied that I didn't think about it at all. We at NCR think of ourselves as a globally competitive company that happens to be headquartered in the United States."[61]

Nations still have important interests and needs, but increasingly have less *economic* ways to secure these. The very concept of a trade crisis is a vestige from earlier eras—like a national appendix (which still can get inflamed). "If companies have the alternative of moving across borders," says Harvard economist Raymond Vernon, "There is not much point in doing a lot of shouting about trade."

Our entire take on national economics & politics needs to be re-evaluated. That applies as much to the Black Nation as to the White Nation.

Go into current u.s.-Japan trade crisis and the "Japan bashing" and "buy American" sentiment that has resulted. What we find as a bottom line is that there isn't much of a trade crisis at all.* What is mistakenly called a trade crisis is really a national crisis for the u.s. as a white settler nation. *Because Japan Inc. and U.S.A. Inc. are gradually merging into one business.* But nobody wants to tell that to the white man, since he's being led around in circles to keep him uselessly occupied. We mean, the Fat Lady is singing, guy.

There is no doubt that "Japan bashing"—which is as amerikkkan as apple pie, anyway—is being socially encouraged. Trade unions and politicians stage smashajapathons, where everyone takes turns sledge hammering some symbolic junker Toyota. Rep. John Dingell (D.–Mich) complains publicly that u.s. autoworkers are victims of those sinister "little yellow men." Popular television bigot Andy Rooney asserts on CBS's "60 minutes":

> "I'm vaguely anti-Japanese. Don't ask me why. Just
> prejudice, I guess. I'm very comfortable with some
> of my prejudices and have no thought of changing
> them now."[62]

The green light is given for racist attacks of any kind on Asians of any kind. Hey, why discriminate.

Only, the ruling class itself isn't joining in, which is why it's so different from the anti-asianism that happened in World War II and the Korean War. No f.b.i. raids on Chinese laundries (it happened a generation ago), no koncentration kamps for Japanese yuppies, since this hysteria is only a bloody circus for bozo. Unnerved by the penetration of Japanese capital up his mainstream, bozo can hardly believe that sacred icons

---

* The u.s. empire has run trade surpluses each year with Western Europe, Afrika, Latin Amerika, and much of Asia. Yet, this never seemed to be a "crisis," unbalanced though it was and is.

of his white culture—such as Columbia movie studios, the
7-11 corporation, and the Rockefeller Center skating rink—
are now Japanese. What's most frustrating of all for Chez
Whitey is that despite having for 12 years elected a right-
wing administration, the Whitest House refused to do
anything against Japan except vomit in the Japanese Prime
Minister's lap ("Look who's coming to dinner!")

The reason for this double-message isn't hard to locate.
Because of the merging and interpenetration of once nation-
ally-separate economies, the State can make public relations
gestures ("trade talks") but has little way to conduct a trade
conflict with Japan that isn't shooting amerikkka in the foot.

Japan, after all, purchased $900 million in u.s. agricul-
tural products in 1991, and is u.s. agri-biz's biggest overseas
customer. Likewise, the u.s. apparel industry sold $400 mil-
lion in favored brands, like levi and ralph lauren, to Japan
last year. Standard Oil and other u.s. petro-chemical corporations own one out of every six gas stations in Japan.
Haagen-Dazs ice cream was recently named one of the ten
most admired products in a Japanese opinion poll (so much
for that supposedly superior Japanese mind). Salomon
Brothers and Morgan Stanley were the second and the third
most profitable brokerage houses in Japan so far this year.[63]
The list would literally fill a phone book.

The concentration of capital overriding national borders
is even more profitably destabilizing to Third World nations.
Not only in merging their production into multinational
commodity trade, but socially, technologically, culturally
as well. The world is being tilted so that the most valuable
ideas, inventions, arts, scientists and technicians fall out of
their nations into the metropolis—or into its Third World
outposts.

The *majority* of PhD. graduate assistants in physics in many u.s. university research laboratories are Chinese (not asian-ams, but from mainland China and Taiwan). Just as the majority of Filipino nurses were educated for years in u.s.-style medical procedures, language and customs—having little to do with the desperate realities of Philippine society—and don't treat other Filipino women but work more profitably in Chicago, Toronto or Lagos. A. Sivanandan finds that his former homeland, Sri Lanka, may be a world production center for computer disc drives, but that the overall consequences of globalization on that small nation have been...

> "...devastating. The oil-rich Gulf States, for
> instance, have sucked in whole sections of the
> working population, skilled and semi-skilled, of
> South Asia, leaving vast holes in the labor structure
> of these countries. Moratuwa, a coastal town in Sri
> Lanka, once boasted some of the finest carpenters
> in the world. Today there are none—they are all
> in Kuwait or in Muscat or Abu Dhabi. And there
> are no welders, masons, electricians, plumbers,
> mechanics—all gone. And the doctors, teachers,
> engineers—they have been long gone—in the first
> wave of postwar migration to Britain, Canada, the
> United States, Australia, in the second wave to
> Nigeria, Zambia, Ghana. Today, Sri Lanka, which
> had the first free health service in the Third World
> and some of the finest physicians and surgeons,
> imports its doctors...all that we are left with in Sri
> Lanka is a plentiful supply of unemployed labor."[64]

***

In concentrating the metropolis and periphery closer together, in moving native production and labor into the imperialist mainstream, neo-colonialism has made the metropolis itself assume a cosmopolitan, multinational character. It has brought the contradictions home to roost, as Malcolm might have said. Indeed, the flow of labor dictated by neo-colonial economics is redrawing our borders. Ruling class-sponsored multiculturalism is a tardy recognition that "America" only lives on in late nite TV reruns. In the N.Y. *Times* book review of David Rieff's new book on Los Angeles—subtitled "Capital of the Third World"—this reality is noted:

> "The old Los Angeles soldiers on in such verdant Westside communities as Brentwood, Bel Air and Pacific Palisades. The new Los Angeles toils on in war zones of ethnic vigilance and random armed visitation in Koreatown and Little El Salvador. Ready or not, says David Rieff, the Los Angeles metropolitan area finds itself 'an anthology of the world,' in transition from the capital of the Sun Belt to the capital of the Third World.

> "By the year 2000, Mr. Rieff notes in 'Los Angeles,' the city will be less than 40 percent white. Already Los Angeles has the second largest populations of Filipinos, Koreans, Mexicans and Salvadorans of any city in the world. Adding, in significant numbers, Chinese, Druze, Ethiopians, Indians, Indonesians, Iranians, Pacific Islanders, Pakistanis,

Tamils, and Vietnamese, Los Angeles is a distinctly cosmopolitan city. Speaking some 82 languages and representing more than 100 ethnic and cultural backgrounds...

"Seeing the city as a preview of the next American century, Mr. Rieff went to Los Angeles from New York City believing that a 'new epoch' had begun. 'Could anyone seriously imagine that changes of this magnitude would leave the United States as it had been before?'"[65]

It is true, white amerikkka and the Third World are like separate planets colliding into each other. For all the drama and the street chaos, this isn't a random mixing. There's a pattern to the fault lines, a structure.

What's going on is a process we can name: de-settlerization. amerikka the empire still legally exists as one nation going into the 21st century, but it's being gradually stripped of its historic identity as a white male settler nation. Los Angeles is not so much "the capital of the Third World", as it is becoming the capital of Aztlan, a re-Latinized and reclaimed Southwest. Not the old peasant Mexico, of course, but some new entity that is both Mexican and part of the multinational Pacific Rim economy. If white folks do the chicken little when a neighborhood "tips", what are they going to do now that their whole nation is "tipping."

This isn't news—or rather, it *is* what's in the news one way or the other almost every day. What white amerikkka makes of it, however, is like "Alien Nation." They believe that the shake n' bake of their country is happening through *external* causes. It comes from *within* u.s. society. As the parasitism which has always characterized settler amerikkka reached a nodal point, in which it began deconstructing the white way of life and the white nation itself. To go into this, we have to discuss the historic tendency within capitalism towards the domination of finance capital.

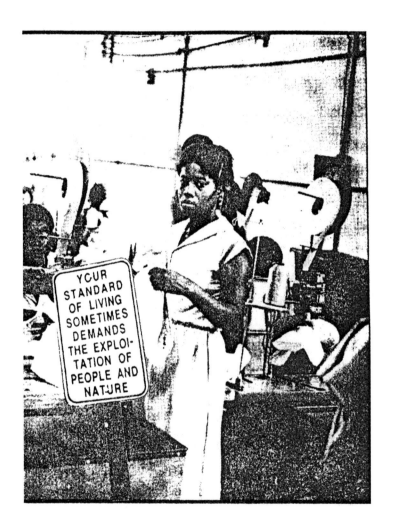

CHAPTER SIX:

THE FUTURE IS NOW

We are breaking through the window of the 21st century just when powerful white men who can't spell as well as 12 year-olds are celebrating the fall of patriarchal socialism, and what they mistakenly think is the triumph of their capitalism. Actually, we are but beginning a new cycle of world struggle. The class struggle between capitalism and the oppressed has only grown larger, more polarized, spilling across old national and racial lines, a world war of a new type. It's easier to talk about it by first taking in the hit that culture gives us.

Ten years ago a hollywood movie named Blade Runner came and went: a modest science-fiction flick, it won some critical acclaim for director Ridley Scott, but wasn't a box office success. Since then, that grade B action film has become an unofficial presence in the larger dimension of politics. Because it resonates with a suppressed truth about amerikkka. Set in the darkly fictional Los Angeles of twenty-five years into the future, Blade Runner contains a take on amerikkka and its non-future that unexpectedly hit a cultural nerve. Now, the phrase "Blade Runner scenario" has crept into mainstream political vocabulary, into white economic conversation, newspaper columns, even books.

On its surface, Blade Runner is a stereotype chase film,

cops and criminals, only set in a future amerikkka. It's that setting, though. In Blade Runner's L.A. even nature has darkened: not the dry sunny freeway days we know, but constant rain and constant street crowds, overcast skies, wet streets. Amerikkka is a Pacificized babel of many races and cultures, a jumble with no set way of life, diet or dress. Standup bars in the middle of pedestrian-jammed streets sell Asian fast food to the working stiffs, and the common language is no longer straight english but a pidgin or a fangala with lots of gestures. An overstrained and tired white men's government tries to keep some kind of public order. No one even mentions what nation it is—that no longer means anything.

Above it all tower the ultra-modern skyscrapers and floating anti-gravity advertising airships of the multinational corporations. Their violent wars over precious raw materials now take place on the outer planets of the solar system, where the minerals are. These wars are fought for them by artificially-produced humans called replicants. Some replicants are workers, miners, or entertainers, while others with their super-human strength and reflexes are designed to be proxy soldiers in the wars between human corporations. As a safety factor for the masters, replicants are built with a short life span and all replicants are banned from the earth's surface outside of the laboratories of the corporations that own them.

The film's hero is Dekker, an LAPD detective (played by hollywood good-guy Harrison Ford, aka Indiana Jones). Dekker knows he's the best at his job, but he also knows that this job is nothing more than being a full-time killer. For Dekker is a "Blade Runner," a special cop whose assignment is to track down and summarily execute escaped slaves, i.e.

replicants. (Stripped of the hi-tech trappings, replicants are only a genetically-created race of slaves). An escaped combat team of four replicants hijack their ship in space and make it to amerikkka, desperately looking for a way to have their lifespans normalized. Dekker's hunt for them, which ends with all four dead (at the end, the last replicant spares Dekker's life without saying why), is the movie's story. Or is it?

However much political economists like Robert B. Reich feel obliged to deny the plausibility of the pessimistic fantasy of the "Blade Runner scenario," it still tugs at them. It keeps being thought of, like a burr stuck in the mind, because this B-movie contains in not-too-disguised forms the truth about amerikkka's neo-colonial future that white people want to keep secret even from themselves. It can be dealt with today only as fiction, as fantasy.

In deconstructing Blade Runner we learn why these secrets (which are only the neo-colonial reality) are both so intriguing and so dangerous that they must be buried.

Blade Runner's future amerikkka is, quite obviously, no longer a white settler nation. Those who run things are still—by historical momentum—white men, but the society they try to hold together is no longer predominantly white or affluent. The culture on the street level is more Third World than it is euro-amerikan. The vision is of the end of amerikkka. This is the side of the "Blade Runner scenario" that attracted so much unofficial attention. But it isn't the only compelling thing about it.

Close in on what is there but unrecognized in the movie: the violated subtext of class and the class structure, as played out in terms of gender, race and nation. This is actually what is at the unspoken center of the scenario.

There is no visible basic economic production in the movie, hardly a mention of it even. Although there are masses of vendors and office people, hi-technicians and street survivors. By implication, basic production (and the primary working class) has been removed not just off-screen but out of society altogether. The dirtiest and most danger-ous work seems to be done off-earth by a lesser race. "Real" people no longer do that work, and the major class division is between their society and the race of less-human beings who do. Sound at all familiar?

It isn't that this film is any brilliant work of art. What's happening is that amerikkka is under tension, twisting between immovable colonial past and inexorable neo-colo-nial future. This society is stressed to the max with neo-colo-nial transformation whose full meaning is still being offi-cially denied. So this suppressed tension—which charges the entire culture now with a certain radical voltage—gets discharged almost at random in popular art, in music, in everything imaginative we do.

And people are drawn unconsciously to the cracks in the censorship of denial. That's why you get a white kid wearing a Public Enemy T-shirt in "Terminator 2," at the same moment Afrikan people are (just like those fictional replicants) declared illegal life forms and are starting to be killed off.

That's the second thing that's missing in Blade Runner's vision of multiculturalized amerikkka—the Afrikan popu-lation has vanished. There are masses of Latins and euro-peans and Asians, but no Afrikans except the occasional extra, the face in the crowd. In the film, even the slave race of replicants is white. The Color Black has been eliminated in fantasy, in "innocently" imagining the future. Truths that cannot be told yet in public, that still must be denied, leak out in imagination, in art.

And, as usual in hollywood, women are present but not as "real" people. There are women characters (every hollywood movie needs women as props to enhance the male leads), but by a subconscious stroke of a scriptwriter's pen in that movie they are all replicants, not "real" humans. The first is a member of the escaped combat team hiding and making her living as a stripper. When Dekker tracks her down, she uses her superior strength to knock him down but only so she can flee. Dekker recovers in time to empty his gun into her back and kill her as she runs down the mall corridor (this white guy is the hero, remember, that we're supposed to identify with). Dekker kills two escaped women slaves and "falls in love" with the last replicant woman, has sex with her, and as the film ends leaves town with her as his exclusive property (i.e. "romance").

When you watch the film in a theater there's no uneasy stirring, no objections from the audience. It's subliminally understood that oppressed women who escape control are menacing, so dangerous to "real" humans that they must be killed. Otherwise, Dekker wouldn't be a "hero", any more than any gestapo investigator was. Hollywood understands without articulating it that gender is really about class and property, too. Truths that cannot be told in public, that must be denied, leak out in art, in imagination. We're talking about class, now.

There isn't anything that unique about the movie. The same truths keep leaking out-largely unnoticed—in other artifacts of sharply changing culture. The television serial "Star Trek: The Next Generation" is popular with the neocolonial generation precisely because it seems so integrated.

Positively multicultural adventures. But look at the closed society of the starship more closely and the subtext says more about multiculturalism than we think. Although the commander is a white man, of course, there are three major parts played by Black actors. One is Jordy, the ship's engineer, a blind man (as in physically sightless) who is mostly concerned with finding technical solutions to his superior's problems ("Yes, we can do it, Captain!") and who has no love life.

The other two characters played by Afrikan actors are actually aliens from two different non-human species (can you interpret that?). So all the characters played by Afrikan actors run around helping white commanders carry out their missions, and since they're of different species they neither reproduce nor form a Black community. This is the same subliminal message as Blade Runner, although in multicultural drag—a future without an Afrikan population. If the mass culture keeps steady sending out this message, what does it mean?

Jump cut to present (which we never left, really).

The "Blade Runner scenario" is so darkly resonant for white men because it's not about a maybe future, it's about what is already going down in the fall of "white America" and the rise of a neo-colonized amerikkka already is becoming a postmodernist jumble, where some white men still run a neo-imperial class structure that is a paradox of modern affluence and human slavery, astonishing technical leaps and growing social barbarism. Akin to the ancient Greece of philosopher and slaves, but on a new and higher level. An empire of a new type. Let's bring that paradox into focus.

AN OVERVIEW OF CLASS

What's happening to the world is that the original class structure of 19th century industrial euro-capitalism as seen in England, the then-leading euro-capitalist nation, has only replicated itself in neo-colonialism—but on a world scale not a national scale, with every feature blown up in size a thousand times.

Industrial England then was like a horror-show of "free enterprise." A hell with people wandering, driven off their lands and homes into industrial zones. Chaotic factories and crude workshops full of slave and semi-slave workers clothed in filthy rags, close to starvation. Many were homeless and sleeping in barracks or next to their machine on the factory floor, living briefly to be used up. This brutal class formation is falsely believed in the white mindset to have been modernized away, smoothed away by progress, but in reality has only been exported, spread and grown more entrenched.

The primitive sweatshops of the garment trade in London and New York never disappeared at all, but have only left the white metropolis and expanded a thousand-fold into Chinatown, El Paso, Haiti, Canton, Bangladesh, Morocco, and South Afrika. The concentrated industry that once made Manchester, England the first great industrial hell has now grown up and left its nuclear family home in the metropolis for Bombay, Korea, Jo'burg, Mexico City, and Brazil. And what were then small pockets of capitalist privilege, green and pleasant upper-class and middle-class neighborhoods in a London or a Boston, have grown to the size of parasitic countries and even semicontinents at the center of a patriarchal world empire of a new type. A center now in crisis.

Classes that once were white or european or male only are now world classes, multinational and in a surface way multicultural. The very high German techno-fetishism of Mercedes-Benz masks the reality that the chromium metal in the alloys are produced by Afrikan workers, that the cars are assembled in part by Turkish emigrant workers, and that Kuwaiti capitalists own one-third of all Mercedes Benz stock.

Much has changed in a century and a half, of course. The cheapened mass production and distribution of commodities has created a dedicated capitalist world. Some sophisticated commodities are universally available in a distorted way. Mexican women in the mass proletarian squatter *colonias* outside El Paso can have walkmans but not running water. In Brazil, 72% of all households have television sets, even though most cannot afford medical care or enough education to read a book—and the right of all men to kill the women they own for any infractions is upheld by law.

To gain an overview of this global class structure, we can start with Egyptian economist Samir Amin's "Class Structure of the Contemporary Imperialist System."[66] While Amin's table is a static view of classes in the euro-centric sense, a surface look, it shows how these classes exist in a world context of center and periphery, oppressor nations and oppressed nations.

While Samir Amin believed that capitalist economics could only be understood by seeing them as parts of one imperialist *system* uniting the periphery and the center/metropolis, he doesn't believe as we do that national economies and national class structures are being absorbed into one world class formation. Nevertheless, when we get to the bottom line of his work the neo-colonial world order comes

A: IMPERIALIST CENTER
(u.s.a., Canada, Western Europe)

Classes	% of world total of economically active adults	% of world total world income
Bourgeoisie & upper middle classes (executives, businessmen, etc.)	7%	40%
Salaried middle class (Amin calls this category of white collar-employees—such as office managers and state civil service staff—the "proletarianized petty-bourgeoisie")	8%	21%
Labor aristocracy (Amin calls this class of foremen, skilled craftsmen in white unions, the "superior working class")	4%	10%
Farmers	3%	6%
Proletariat (factory laborers, migrant farm workers, domestics, service employees like messengers and porters, street vendors and day laborers—or "inferior working class" in Amin's terminology)	4%	6%
TOTAL	26%	83%

B: IMPERIALIST PERIPHERY
(Afrika, Asia, Middle East, Oceana, Latin Amerika)

Classes	% of world total of economically active adults	% of world total world income
Native bourgeoisie & upper middle classes	1%	5%
Salaried middle class	6%	2%
Proletariat	4%	1%
Landowning farmers, including landlords	4%	2%
Middle peasants	11%	2%
Poor peasants	44%	4%
TOTAL	70%	6%

Amin's class breakdown is only approximate, of course, because he had to use capitalist census data. The breakdown into classes is simplified, to say the least. It is also two decades old in terms of data, and while it is still useful it doesn't reflect the massive population shift in the Imperialist Periphery from the peasant countryside to the cities, and the growth of all urban classes. This population total does not equal 100% because we omitted his category of official unemployed (4%), which is only misleading. Total world income percentages do not equal 100% because of rounding off.

into *class* focus on a larger-than-national basis.

The central feature of imperialism during the colonial period was that it created entire parasitic societies by forcibly polarizing the world into oppressor and oppressed nations, and this continues to be true under neo-colonialism. *Neo-colonialism is, incredibly enough, in some ways even more parasitic in its effects than colonialism was.* This is driving world political contradictions to a new level.

In the neo-imperial metropolis, *all* classes of citizens receive a greater percentage of the world's income than their share in the population, as Samir Amin shows. An important exception we must note—because Amin's table doesn't recognize it—are those peoples in the metropolis that capitalism has marginalized and set aside from its economy to be exterminated. Capitalists and their upper middle class managers and technicians are only 8% of the world's population (capitalists alone are under 1%), but take 45% of all world income.

This explains why there's an emerging pattern of global yuppie culture: of privileged people who speak the same computer languages, own similar property, have identical financial skills, who wear the same Armani or Perry Ellis clothes to work for the same multinational corporations in different continents, and whose children may well intermarry across old racial, national, and gender lines. "Class is everything."

And, on the other hand, why there's an opposite *class* pattern emerging of homeless Afrikan street children being targets of violent elimination not only in the slums of Brazil, but around the globe—in Panama City, Nairobi, Kenya, in islamic Sudan, and in Brooklyn, too. This civilization that has space walks above the earth and genetically altered cells reinjected to fight tumors, is with equal sophistication set-ting it up for surplus Afrikan children to be hunted like game animals. Or do you still think it's all coincidences?

When we said earlier that the commodity life of the capi-talist system is nothing like we think it is, that's equivalent to saying that the class structure is nothing like we think it is, also. **To a remarkable extent, the class analysis of 19th century industrial euro-capitalism done by Karl Marx is still true today,** although this can only be grasped by overturning euro-centrism (which in this instance can be discovered as being co-terminus with patriarchy) and seeing, with fresh eyes, the world as a whole.

As useful as the broad statistical foundation given us by Amin is, suggesting many things, its limitations become evi-dent once we confront Black Genocide or the oppression of women as property. The question is not a mere inequality between occupational groupings, some richer, some poorer, as reformers like to believe. The imperialist class structure is actually a living machinery, of clashing relationships to pro-duction, whose essential fuel is capital extracted by genocide, by slavery and dispossession and looting on a mass scale. Not as dead history, but right now.

We have to bring up into full view the hidden center of the capitalist machinery—the processes that Marx first sci-entifically identified as *primitive accumulation* and the link between *semi-slavery* and *"slavery pure and simple."*

Our primary question is, who is the modern proletariat and what role does it play as a class? The answer is simple: it is primarily women, children, and alien labor. Those who are colonized. The modern proletariat or industrial working class, which is both among the most oppressed and the most productive class that supports the structure of capitalist society by its labor, is not and has never been gender-neutral or nationally self-contained. No matter how indignantly some men may scream at these words, this is a matter of historical record, of fact.

In its infancy, the first English factory system of the 18th century was like a chain of prison workhouses, whose semi-slave laborers were primarily women and enslaved children. English men, no matter how poor, resisted giving up what independence they had to become "like women." A *class* attitude using gender, race and nation in a way that the dominant values of the British ruling class encouraged. British historian Christopher Hill reminds his reader that being a factory worker was so disrespectable a position back then that it virtually placed *her* outside society, as an alien, a non-citizen (the word "worker" today is supposed to make us think "him", the blue collar unionized man in heavy industry, so we misunderstand economics and class). Hill wrote:

> "We look back with twentieth-century preconceptions. After two hundred years of trade union struggle, wage labour has won a respected and self-respecting position in the community. But if we approach wage-labour from the seventeenth century, as men in fact did, we recall that the Levellers thought wage-labourers had forfeited their birthright as freeborn Englishmen, and should not be allowed to vote; that Winstanley thought wage-labourers had no share in their own country, and that wage labour should be abolished. This traditional attitude, together with the fact that many factories looked like workhouses, and were often consciously modelled on them (paupers

too had been thought unworthy of the franchise
by the Levellers) may help us to understand why
independent craftsmen clung so hard to economically untenable positions; why the early Lancashire
spinning factories were staffed *so largely by women
and pauper children,* the latter of whom had no
choice in the matter, and by Welsh and Irish
laborers (Highlanders in Scotland), who lacked
the English craftsman's tradition of self-help and
self-respect…."[67]

Isn't it typical that Hill, a "Marxist" historian, says that Welsh
and Irish and Scotch men worked as women did in the early
factories when English men still didn't have to—because
they supposedly "lacked the English craftsman's tradition of
self-help and self-respect"—but fails to mention that those
non-English men were *colonial subjects* of England, then. In
its very origins, the industrial proletariat was a *colonized* class,
in which alien men without rights were *equal* to women and
children without rights.

That Oxford professor "just doesn't get it", as the saying
goes. On the very next paragraph of his book, after admitting
that early English factory workers were primarily women
and children, Hill reverts to discussing working people as
"he", "his", "men", and "workingmen."

While professor Hill doesn't admit the importance of
children's labor to capitalism, he does briefly tell of their
exploitation in the early factory:

"Pauper children shipped north from London
workhouses in order to save ratepayers the cost of
their maintenance were particularly unprotected.

From the age of seven children in factories had to
work twelve to fifteen hours a day (or night), six
days a week, 'at best in monotonous jail, at worst
in a hell of human cruelty.' 'The tale never ended
of fingers cut off and limbs crushed in the wheels.'
Foremen's wages depended on the work they could
get out of their charges. The story of these children
is, as Professor Ashton mildly remarks, 'a depress-
ing one.'"[68]

This historic development of the modern capitalist proletariat, a class that is predominantly women and children,
took place in Europe within the furnaces of what Karl Marx
termed *primitive accumulation*. That is, the *first* accumulation of capital that allows the capitalist class to make invest-
ments, to first become itself. Their own mythology that
capitalism derived its first stake through the would-be capitalist's prudent savings and self-denial is, of course, about as
real as Santa Claus. Marx, in his investigation of the inner
workings of the capitalist system, identified primitive accumulation as "the expropriation of the immediate producers,
i.e., the dissolution of private property based on the labor of
its owner."[69] By which he meant the "free" looting and violent
seizure of lands and slaves by capitalism that took place first
inside Europe, and then outward in ever-widening circles of
colonialism, in particular Indian and Afrikan slavery.

We know, of course, what Marx did not. That the process
of primitive accumulation in Europe began with the "inner
colony," the enslavement of women and children as human
property. In the long witchhunts from the 13th through the
18th centuries, in which millions of european women were
terrorized and killed, the emerging capitalist nation-states

established their ownership of women as men's property. To do unwaged labor and to have their bodies used to reproduce still greater surpluses of cheap labor-power as the State willed it.

How natural, then, for women and children, who were not "real" human beings (just as those disposable replicants in Blade Runner), to be the primary labor force to be used up. And as industry began, a *generalized* violent primitive accumulation took hold in England, in which euro-capitalism dispossessed millions of peasants from their traditional farmlands (just as it did in Northern Mexico—aka California, New Mexico, Texas, Arizona, Colorado—in the 1830s–1870s, in South Afrika and Zimbabwe in the early 1900s, and Chile in the 1970s) to create both large commercial agricultural estates and masses of desperate, homeless wage-laborers to be hired cheaply. Historian Christopher Hill reminds his reader that the coming of industry has always been accompanied by a lowering of living standards for the oppressed classes, while the middle and upper classes benefited:

> "In England the general price level rose five times between 1530 and 1640, wheat prices six times. This had a dual effect. First, since English prices lagged behind those of the Continent, there was a great stimulus to cloth exports in the years 1530 to 1550; and though the boom broke in the latter year, a considerable degree of prosperity continued.

"Second, there was a savage depression of the living
standards of the lower half of the population, since
food and fuel prices rose more sharply than those
of other commodities. In the building industry real
wages in the later sixteenth century were less than
two-thirds of what they had been in 1510, and in
the fifty years before the civil war they were less
than half. The mass of the population was forced
down to a diet of black bread. For those who possessed no land this was a catastrophe. For those
with land but who produced little or nothing for
the market, it meant that wives and children were
forced to by-earning in the clothing industry. Some
time between 1580 and 1617 the word 'spinster'
acquired its modern sense of unmarried woman:
for of course such a woman would have to spin.
Competition was so great that female wages rose
even less than male in the late sixteenth and early
seventeenth centuries.

" ... In the last two decades of the sixteenth century, and again in the depressed sixteen-twenties,
preachers and pamphleteers talk of men, women
and children dying of starvation in the streets of
London.

"The conception of rising population, monetary
inflation and declining real wages may be difficult
for those to grasp who think in terms of modern
economic models. But in this pre-industrial society
much of the labor force was employed only part-
time, much labour was semi-forced."[70]

Hill, writing from the vantage point of Oxford and the metropolis, has the eurocentric view that this extreme exploitation was only what early capitalism had to do to get rolling. His words seem like irony to us today, since "men, women and children dying of starvation in the streets" is a very up-to-date and worldwide phenomenon. It has only been exported to the oppressed world. And those who have lived under Reagan and Thatcher have no trouble understanding "the conception of rising population, monetary inflation and declining real wages ..."

"Semi-forced" labor and slavery is also a major phenomenon still on a world scale. Just ask the many thousands of Afrikan women slaves who are regularly bought and sold today, both for sex and unwaged labor, by their captors in the islamic Sudan (whose slavemaster government is the leading Afrikan ally of islamic Iran). Or the thousands of Thai women slaves in the Bangkok brothels for the Western-Japanese tourist industry.

The point here is that primitive accumulation has never stopped, was not just a beginning, and that it has a specific gender and national character. Today we use the phrase "wage slave" as self-deprecating humor, but in its origins it was meant literally: someone who was hired for a wage but was really a semi-slave. Marx described how the gender character of capitalist industry was intrinsic to its nature, moving from there to the hidden dependence of "veiled slavery" of the industrial proletariat on the naked slavery of the Afrikan slave trade:

> "In England women are still occasionally used
> instead of horses for hauling canal boats, because
> the labour required to produce horses and

machines is an accurately known quantity, while
that required to maintain the women of the
surplus-population is below all calculation. Hence
nowhere do we find a more shameful squandering
of human labour-power for the most despicable
purposes than in England, the land of machinery…

"In so far as machinery dispenses with muscular
power, it becomes a means of employing labour-
ers of slight muscular strength, and those whose
bodily development is incomplete, but whose limbs
are all the more supple. The labour of women and
children was, therefore, the first thing sought for
by capitalists who used machinery. That mighty
substitute for labor and laborers was forthwith
changed into a means for increasing the number of
wage-labourers by enrolling, under the direct sway
of capital, every member of the workman's family,
without distinction of age or sex.

"Machinery also revolutionises out and out the
contract between the labourer and the capitalist,
which formally fixes their mutual relations. Taking
the exchange of commodities as our basis, our first
assumption was that capitalist and labourer met
as free persons, as independent owners of commodities; the one possessing money and means of
production, the other labour-power. But now the
capitalist buys children and young persons under
age. Previously, the workman sold his own labour-
power, which he disposed of nominally as a free
agent. Now he sells wife and child. He has become
a slave-dealer.

"The demand for children's labour often resembles
in form the inquiries for negro slaves, such as were
formerly to be read among the advertisements in
American journals. 'My attention,' says an English
factory inspector, 'was drawn to an advertisement in
the local paper of one of the most important manufacturing towns of my district, of which the following is a copy: Wanted, 12 to 20 young persons, not
younger than what can pass for 13 years. Wages,
4 shillings a week. Apply &c.' The phrase 'what can
pass for 13 years,' has reference to the fact, that
by the Factory Act, children under 13 years may
work only 6 hours. A surgeon officially appointed
must certify their age. The manufacturer, therefore,
asks for children who look as if they were already
13 years old. The decrease, often by leaps and
bounds in the number of children under 13 years
employed in factories, a decrease that is shown in
an astonishing manner by the English statistics of
the last 20 years, was for the most part, according
to the evidence of the factory inspectors themselves,
the work of the certifying surgeons, who overstated
the age of the children, agreeably to the capitalist's
greed for exploitation, and the sordid traffick-
ing needs of the parents. In the notorious district
of Bethnal Green, a public market is held every
Monday and Tuesday morning, where children of
both sexes from 9 years of age upwards, hire themselves out to the silk manufacturers."[71] [...]

"With the development of capitalist production
during the manufacturing period, the public

opinion of Europe had lost the last remnant of
shame and conscience. The nations bragged cyni-
cally of every infamy that served them as a means
to capitalistic accumulation. Read, e.g., the naive
Annals of Commerce of the worthy A. Anderson.
Here it is trumpeted forth as a triumph of English
statecraft that at the Peace of Utrecht, England
extorted from the Spaniards by the Asiento Treaty
the privilege of being allowed to ply the negro-trade,
until then only carried on between Africa and the
English West Indies, between Africa and Spanish
America as well. England thereby acquired the
right of supplying Spanish America until 1743 with
4,800 negroes yearly. This threw, at the same time,
an official cloak over British smuggling. Liverpool
waxed fat on the slave-trade.

"This was its method of primitive accumulation.
And, even to the present day, Liverpool 'respectabil-
ity' is the Pindar of the slave-trade which—compare the work of Aikin [1795] already quoted—
'has coincided with the spirit of bold adventure
which has characterized the trade of Liverpool and
rapidly carried it to its present state of prosperity;
has occasioned vast employment for shipping and
sailors, and greatly augmented the demand for the
manufactures of the country' (p. 339). Liverpool
employed in the slave-trade, in 1730, 15 ships; in
1751, 53; in 1760, 74; in 1770, 96; and in 1792, 132.

"Whilst the cotton industry introduced child-
slavery in England, it gave in the United States a
stimulus to the transformation of the earlier, more

or less patriarchal slavery, into a system of commercial exploitation. **In fact, the veiled slavery of the
wage-workers in Europe needed, for its pedestal,
slavery pure and simple in the new world ...**

" ... If money, according to Augier,'comes into the
world with a congenital blood-stain on one cheek,'
capital comes dripping from head to foot, from
every pore, with blood and dirt."[72]

We can have a deeper take on Marx's observations than Marx
himself had, because of the added vantage points of the
anti-colonial revolutions and the rise of women's liberation.
Early in the 20th century Rosa Luxemburg, a Polish-Jewish
revolutionary who was considered among the most brilliant
socialist theoreticians in Europe, was trying to understand
why euro-capitalism had never collapsed economically as
Marx had predicted. Her insight was that the great flow of
"free" capital from primitive accumulation had, in fact, never
stopped enriching the system.

In her 1912 book, *Accumulation of Capital*, Rosa
Luxemburg argued that euro-capitalism had remained vig-
orous only through the constant conquest and looting of
colonial and semi-colonial peoples, whether inside Europe
or "the wretched Indian victims in Putamayo, the Negroes
in Africa..."[73] Due to Luxemburg's her-esy, both in being a
strong-minded woman and her moving the theoretical focus
of anti-capitalist economics outside Europe to the Third
World, her insights were ignored among white people for
half a century—until European radical feminists recovered
her thought.

PRIMITIVE ACCUMULATION MASKED AS "CHARITY"

The neo-colonial class structure is to a large degree unseen, off-screen, hidden not only by global distance but by willful social camouflage. Southern Afrika is an example. Most white people really believe that Afrika is just a vast charity case, of backward peoples who can't even feed themselves. Now, euro-charities are reporting "burnout," that even with those glitzy "We Are The World" concerts and videos, white middle-class consumers are tired of giving spare change endlessly to feed Afrikans. Isn't that true?

Oddly enough, before euro-capitalism came to "aid" Southern Afrika the living standard there was one of basic abundance. Most Afrikans lived better in 1600 than they do now in 1992. Hunger and certainly famine were not common. When the first white explorers and settlers came to Zimbabwe in the 1890s they were shocked—the *Afrikans were living better than most people did back in Europe.* You can see what an emergency that was, and how capitalism had to send in troops to stop that. Historian T.O. Ranger, writing about the Shona peoples (the broad linguistic-cultural group that is the majority population in Zimbabwe and part of Mozambique), tells us:

> "That Shona were everywhere cultivators rather than pastoralists. And their agriculture was a rich one. Over the centuries the Zambezi valley had received crops from outside Africa and diffused them to other areas. By the nineteenth century the Shona could make use of wide variety of crop types. Thus the first white settlers in Melsetter in 1893 listed 'mealies, poko corn, kafir

corn, millet, ground-nuts, beans (five sorts), egg
fruit, cabbages, tomatoes, peas, pumpkins of sorts,
water-melons, cucumbers, sweet potatoes, chillies,
tobacco, bananas and lemons, and all these grown
to perfection'. At the same time an early settler in
western Mashonaland was describing the successful and varied agriculture of chief Mashiangombi's
people. 'The path wound through fields of mealies,
kafir corn, rukwasza, sweet potatoes, pumpkins,
peanuts, and then across rice-beds in the marshes';
cattle and goats were herded; and game abounded
to provide further fresh meat. All Shona were
involved in this cultivation except specialists in the
arts of government and religion. Then men cleared
the ground and together with the women planted,
weeded and harvested. The young men also hunted,
usually in communal groups. This Shona agriculture proved readily capable of expanding to meet
the demands of the new white population after
1890 and for the first ten years at least the whites
depended upon it for the greater part of their food
supply.

"A number of crafts flourished among the Shona—
white observers claimed in the 1880s that Shona
technical skills were 'really astonishing' and that
the Shona stood first 'in the industrial arts of a
rudimentary civilization' of all the tribes south of
the Zambezi. Cloth was woven from wild cotton
or bark fibre; elaborate and highly ornamented
pottery was made; at court centres like Zimbabwe
and Khami there developed carving in ivory and

soapstone and a skillful use of gold for decorative
purposes—gold beads, gold wire, paper-thin gold
plates to cover models of animals. The Shona were
skilled iron workers and produced hoes, hatchets,
spears, arrows, and so on.

"Internal trade was well developed. Shona groups
specially skillful in iron working or close to rich
deposits of ore would barter iron goods for cloth or
tobacco with other Shona peoples ...."[74]

Now, one hundred years after capitalism arrived in Southern
Afrika, hunger and starvation are very real problems. Far
from having "developed", Afrika has in relative world terms
slid backwards. The whole of Black Afrika, with its population of over 500 millions, has an annual gross national product or GNP *less* than that of New York City alone.[75] There is
a *dis*-accumulation of capital going on. The reason has to do
with raging primitive accumulation in modern form.

We are deeply, intimately involved in Afrika. Much more
than we let ourselves know. Because of one of the world's
biggest charities. That charity ball where each year Afrikans
have to give billions of dollars worth of goods as gifts to
amerikkka. Imperialism runs this charity drive, only it's
Afrikans who are the real givers and most "Americans" who
are the real recipients. That is why the u.s. government
wants Stepin' Fetchit singing "We are the World," why they
need all those do-gooding white relief agencies talking that
talk about feeding Afrika. *To keep hidden the fact that it is
amerikkka that feeds on Afrika.*

Take South Afrika. Which is easy to read, if you really
want to. For isn't the amerikkkan dream intravenously connected to South Afrika? What is nuclear love without a

diamond engagement ring? Millions and millions of bondage insignia with DeBeers diamonds from South Afrika.
Isn't that fitting? The u.s. mint has been selling investment-
grade gold coins, the "u.s. eagle." 80% of the gold in the "eagle"
is purchased from the Anglo-American corporation, South
Afrika's largest gold and minerals producer. Uncle Sam, the
pimp, wants to help us personally invest in South Afrikan
exploitation. Oh, and those exotic flowers at the wedding
might have come from South Afrika, too. Cleverly repack-
aged and transhipped, of course, in Holland and Israel. Even
the u.n. in New York, it turns out, has been buying South
Afrikan flowers for its lobby.

When you cruise down the expressway in your Japanese
car, your Toyota or Nissan or whatever, it doesn't matter to
you that its steel was made from South Afrikan iron ore. It
doesn't matter when you pull up for gasoline at the nearest
Shell or Exxon station, that South Afrikan platinum was
used in the refining process as a catalyst. Or that the same
South Afrikan platinum was needed for your long distance
telephone call (to make the fiber optic telephone lines). Or
that South Afrikan chromium and vanadium was necessary
for the "super-alloy" jet engines that propel your United air-
liner across the continent at 30,000 feet. Or that the wheat
cracker you snack on during the flight was grown with
chemical fertilizers that require South Afrikan rare metals
as catalysts during production, and harvested with a John
Deere combine whose steel body and engine required South
Afrikan manganese and chromium.

No, it doesn't matter to us at all that this way of life has
an addiction to Soweto.

According to a u.s. commerce department study, South
Afrika supplies 50% of all the platinum used in the u.s., 39%

of the manganese, 44% of the vanadium, and 55% of the chromium.[76] Reporting on their industrial dependence on African minerals, the *N.Y. Times* wrote:

> "A total lack of these metals would shut down or throttle the steel, automotive, chemical, plastics and petroleum industries. It would halt the production of optical fiber for the communications industry. It would severely hobble the production of food, com-puter components and weapons.

> "The effects on an industrialized nation of a loss of chromium were indicated in a 1978 West German study, which concluded that a shortfall of only 30 percent of the metal for one year would result in a one-quarter reduction of West Germany's total goods and services."[77]

In practical terms, the middle-class way of life, perhaps even the overall living standard, would undergo an instant decompression if deprived of the products of Afrika's land and labor. Or if they had to pay for them. For capitalism's secret is that they get it for free. With one exception.

There is no trade here, not even "unequal trade", for the transaction is all one way. That's why the labor is slave and semi-slave. In the life of the average South Afrikan worker there is absolutely nothing from far-off amerikkka, with one exception. She raises her children (the next genera-tion's factory workers, miners and domestics) on the dusty, marginal lands that the white farmers didn't want, doing a meager subsistence farming. Or else she is a factory worker, or a domestic servant for the settler women, living alone in a tiny shack behind their u.s. style house. Or he is a miner living for a lifetime in a crowded barracks, sleeping on a bare concrete shelf, stacked three high. Their diet is largely grain meal porridge, unleavened baked meal cakes, and some vegetables. Part of the men's cash is spent on alcohol and tobacco. Real things from amerikka—fancy consumer products and medical technology and cars—are completely beyond their means.

What u.s. society gives them in return for the strategic metals, the gold and diamonds, the outpouring that sustains the neo-imperial way of life is... *white people's old, used, cast-off clothing.* That is the only amerikkkan commodity they get. A report on the recent business pages noted:

> "'A guy makes $200 a year, so how can he afford
> new clothes?' said Edward Stubin, a used-clothing
> exporter from Greenpoint, Brooklyn, smiling
> contentedly. By some estimates one third of the 470
> million people in sub-Saharan Africa are walk-
> ing around in cast-off European and American
> clothing."[78]

Discarded clothing is sold by the pound, ten cent or twenty cent a pound, by the Salvation Army, Goodwill and other businesses that collect them. The exporters then disinfect it, plastic wrap it in 100 pound bales, and ship it all over the Third World to be resold to local merchants and peddlers. This is one of amerikkka's main exports to the Third World. Across Black Afrika you can see people wearing white peoples' discarded T-shirts, dresses, jeans, coats, blouses, and pants.

The article mentions that: "Mr Stubin, president of Trans-Americas FSG Inc., ships about 10 million pounds of used clothing a year from New York, mainly to Africa. Even with so big a volume, he considers himself only 'one of the top 10' American exporters to Africa."

They say that Afrika's strategic metals are "irreplaceable." It is more truthful to say that the price is right.

Experimental automobile engines made of ceramic instead of high-strength steel work fine, for example, but cost $10,000 a piece. Which is why no one is rushing to buy them yet. Manganese can be mined by dredging up ore nodules from the ocean floor. At great expense, as we can tell from the fact that the French are investing $770 million in just one pilot project to get manganese from the Mediterranean bottom. As for chromium, they can always get all the chromium they need from low-grade ore on the Indian Nations in Montana. At about five to ten times the current cost. As the *N.Y. Times* pointed out, "One smelter would consume about a million watts of electricity an hour, a staggering expense for the manufacturer or the government."[79]

But in South Afrika, these precious commodities are given to imperialism for free. While the u.s. has to pay something for South Afrikan commodities, this has only represented the costs of maintaining the white settler population and their police state, so that capitalism's reverse charity goes on. In other "independent" Afrikan states, that same cost represents kickbacks to the local Black elite and *their* police state, so that the charity goes on and on.

There is a simple equation that sums up your intimate relationship with South Afrika. That untangles all the export-import-capital-investment-blah-blah algebra. They, Afrikan workers, give amerikkka their great natural resources and lifetimes of hard labor to make your consuming society work, free of charge, as an involuntary gift. We, on our part, to make the equation balance, give them death and misery. Your way of life only grows like an exotic hot-house vine from their deaths, which is something more intimate than any romance.

When we follow the intravenous connection full of blood between amerikkkan dreams and the dusty streets of Soweto, we descend into an underworld. There, in the lower depths beneath our skyscraper society, we can at last see the vast machinery that burns day and night to support your way of life. The machinery is named genocide. Which is why the real class structure of the world must remain hidden, unseen.

THE INDUSTRIAL PROLETARIAT:
GENDER & RACE, SLAVE & SEMI-SLAVE

That the postmodern capitalist proletariat is predominantly oppressed women and children is, of course, a her-etical thought, literally unthinkable in the neo-colonized view of the world. To socially camouflage this class formation it has not only been placed over the horizon from white society, but an *artificial ideology* of work has been implanted in our consciousness. It goes like this: The labor that men do—particularly euro-men—is the important macho work, whether it's building jet airplanes or designing shopping malls. The labor that women do reproducing the human race, feeding it and clothing it ("light industry"), is feminine and less important, economically very secondary. The labor that children do in this false consciousness is invisible and trivial, so insignificant it can be completely brushed aside and need not even be considered as part of the world economy. Forgotten completely. For children, after all, are even less "real" humans than women are.

When we said that the class structure of the neo-colonial world is like the 19th century industrial euro-capitalism as Marx analyzed it, only expanded a thousand times to a world scale, we weren't just speaking metaphorically. Marx, for example, spent many pages in his major work, *Capital*, describing the importance of children's labor to industrial capitalism. Children who were, he makes clear, really slaves sold into bondage by their families or "guardians." He was particularly indignant that these children, the least powerful persons in society, were knowingly forced into dangerous and toxic industries as cheap and disposable slave labor:

> "The manufacture of lucifer matches dates from 1833, from the discovery of the method of applying phosphorus to the match itself. Since 1845 this manufacture has rapidly developed in England, and has extended especially amongst the thickly populated parts of London as well as in Manchester, Birmingham, Liverpool, Bristol, Norwich, Newcastle and Glasgow. With it has spread the form of lockjaw, which a Vienna physician in 1845 discovered to be a disease peculiar to lucifer-matchmakers. Half the workers are children under thirteen, and young persons under eighteen. The manufacture is on account of its unhealthiness and unpleasantness in such bad odor that only the most miserable part of the labouring class, half-starved widows and so forth, deliver up their children to it, 'the ragged, half-starved, untaught children.'

"Of the witnesses that Commissioner White examined (1863), 270 were under 18, 50 under 10, 10 only 8, and 5 only 6 years old. A range of the working-day from 12 to 14 or 15 hours, night-labour, irregular meal-times, meals for the most part taken in the very workrooms that are pestilent with phosphorus. Dante would have found the worst horrors of his Inferno surpassed in this manufacture."[80]

Isn't it good that capitalist civilization has moved beyond these criminal relations of production, and that matchstick production is now done in safely automated factories? That is everyone's metropolitan assumption, although no one you ask will actually know how matches are made. From a news dispatch out of New Delhi, India—not in 1889 but 1989:

"These are the dark ages for millions of children in Southeast Asia who eat slop, sleep in hovels, and work in dim, airless factories. They are slaves—illiterate, intimidated, ruthlessly exploited.

"Eleven year-old Chinta, from India's Tamil Nadu state, rides a company bus to a matchstick factory before dawn and makes 40 cents for a ten-hour shift.

"'Some of the children have the breathing sickness and eye disease because of the chemicals,' she said.

"Uma Shankun, 12, weaves exquisite Persian carpets in the northern Indian state of Uttar Pradesh for Western buyers. His mother and two sisters [also] work in the factory to help pay off the family's $30 loan, taken after his father died.

"Uma said they tried to escape once, but were beaten.

"More than 20 million children in Southeastern Asia are in 'chains of servitude' and millions more are working in conditions similar to slavery, a conference on child servitude concluded this month.

"Most of them are outcasts or untouchables, tribal or religious minorities.

"They are 'non-beings, exiles of civilization, living a life worse than that of animals,' P.N. Bhagwati, India's former chief justice, told the conference.

"The cheap labor that developing countries tout to lure foreign investment is often a child's, human rights campaigner Krishnaiyer told the conference."[81]

These 20 million child slaves in Southeast Asia are not merely exploited, they are involuntary laborers, physically held in bondage by some capitalist they have been sold to or are in perpetual debt to. The word "slave" is used literally and exactly here.

At Macy's department store in Manhattan, investigators found five square yard Moroccan carpets bearing the proud label, "Made in Morocco exclusively for R.H. Macy's." But who actually made this carpet? It turns out that her name is Hiyat and she is 11 years old.

"RABAT—Perched on a low wooden bench in front of a loom, cutting knife at her side, Hiyat is an automaton with whirring hands.

"At the age of 11, Hiyat knots rugs six days a week in a concrete box where 200 weavers hunch elbow to elbow at hand looms. Forty years ago carpet weaving was a handicraft that little Moroccan girls learned at home from their mothers. Now it is big business and little girls as young as 4 work in factories.

"*Loop, wrap, pull, slice. Loop, wrap, slice.* Hiyat would have to tie one strand of woolen pile onto the loom every 2.43 seconds to keep up with what her supervisor says is the factory's pace of knotting. The monotony tears on her. 'I wanted to stay in school,' she said, 'not work here.'

"The factory that hired her, Mocary SA, is part of a global shame. Tens of thousands of well-to-do employers throughout the Third World work children for pennies an hour in mind-blunting or dangerous jobs. Others make money by maneuvering children into criminal work, turning homeless boys into street thieves or 13 year-old girls into prostitutes.

"We prefer to get them when they are about seven," said Nasser Yebbous, the overseer of one plant in Marrakesh. Children's hands are nimbler, he said. "And their eyes are better, too. They are faster when they are small."[82]

Under piecework rates, Hiyat earns at most 15 cents an hour in Morocco. Halfway around the world, Eliza Lualhati, 15, says she earns about 13 cents an hour for piecemeal work at a high-speed sewing machine in a live-in garment factory in a suburb of Manila. Eliza doesn't complain about working 90 to 110 hours a week. But she said she wishes the boss wouldn't make her pay for the thread.

Eliza's routine six days a week at the War Win's Style shirt factory goes like this: Wake up at 6 a.m. on a pile of cloth scraps beside her sewing machine. Make breakfast. Sweep the sewing room floor. Then:

> "We start sewing exactly at 7 a.m. We usually get a break around noon. It lasts maybe two hours, but only half an hour if we are on a rush. We start up again for the afternoon and work until about 7 p. m. We stop for about half an hour for dinner.

> "Then we start sewing again. Usually until midnight. Sometimes it is until 3 a.m. In December, we go right on through, just taking a catnap."

The factory owner, Josie Cruz, sounded compassionate. "Sometimes they get ill," she said. "Some of them have suffered anemia from lack of sleep."

But Cruz said if she wants to succeed in the garment business, she has no choice. "We have a strict shipping schedule," she said. "If we fail to deliver, there will be no work to be done for the next two weeks. So whenever there is a rush order, they know they have to finish, even if they have to work 23 hours a day."

Wages are even lower in Thailand, where thousands of young peasant girls work seven days a week inside hole-in-the-wall Bangkok factories called "shophouses" for less than seven cents an hour…"Sometimes I don't get a day off for weeks," said Sarapa Nasap, who wraps toy Uzi machine guns in a plastics factory in Bangkok.

Sarapa, 15, said she is paid a monthly salary of $20, plus a bonus of 20 cents each night she works later than 10 p.m. Spread out over the 70 to 90 hours a week she says she works, her pay would average six cents an hour.

Among nine Bangkok sweatshop children whom reporters succeeded in interviewing away from their bosses, the pay ranged from 3 to 16 cents an hour.

The live-in factory system is such an accepted part of Thailand's labor patterns that it didn't embarrass one of Sarapa's bosses to talk about the arrangements.

"If we give them meals, then we can control them very easily," said Komol Trairattanapa, export manager of Siam Asian Enterprises Ltd.

When euro-amerikkkans hear these facts, they oh and ah in pretended surprise and pity. And then forget about it that minute. "It's shocking," people say, or "It's a disgrace that these countries don't protect their children." But really, it's just your daily life, just the only way that your capitalism has ever done business from day one. It's no more unusual or shocking than the fact that for a white woman to go to medical school and become a doctor, several Afrikkan women must die to pay for it.

We put it that way deliberately, to bring your mind up short. White women in particular assume that their careers are only a positive thing for the world. But since white culture doesn't support itself, doesn't produce its own daily necessities, every breath that white women take costs somebody else something. Revolutionary women have pointed out that the food white women eat was taken from a Third World woman's mouth; the clothing their children wear was taken from a Third World child's back. Since it costs over $200,000 a year above and beyond that to educate a u.s.

medical student, many women in the Third World must be robbed of necessities of life to pay the bill. White men don't pay it, that's for sure.

Then, too, white women join a euro-capitalist medical industry that has always fed off the suffering of Third World women. The "great" pioneer of u.s. gynecology, Dr. James Marion Sims of Montgomery, Alabama, developed his operation curing vesico vaginal fistula (caused by torn tissue during childbirth) by experimenting on Afrikan slave women. By the time he succeeded in 1849, Dr. Sims had operated on one slave woman (whose owner had named her "Anarcha") some thirty times. Thirty times—can you picture what that was for her? In our lifetimes, "the pill" for birth control was first tested for dosages and side-effects on some 15,000 unknowing Puerto Rican women. Just as when French AIDS researchers, working with the u.s. National Institutes of Health, wanted to test a hoped-for AIDS vaccine for safety, they flew to Zaire and injected healthy Afrikan children with their concoction.

We must reject the ideology of euro-charities and social work bureaucracies that children are special, are somehow precious and must be protected. Whenever anyone says that, how this group or that group is special and needs protecting, that only means that they own you. That only means that you're property. When they're free, animals don't need the SPCA. Check it out.

In the capitalist world order every national government is supposed to protect its citizens, men are supposed to protect women, and adults are supposed to protect children. But nowhere in the world is this true. The supposed need to "protect" is really the ideological justification for keeping you powerless so you can be abused and exploited. Children aren't special, aren't precious, like patriarchal capitalism likes to pretend; they're just people.

Remember when vp Dan Quayle attacked the tv character Murphy Brown for being an unwed mother. The next day his staff flew him to California, so he could hold a press conference in a captive barrio junior high school to talk his "family values" lies. Afterwards, one Chicana student in that classroom told the media:"I don't want to bag the vice-president or anything, but he has a mentality just like mine only I'm 14 years old. Which would you rather have, a single mother or a father who gets drunk and beats your mother?"

Millions could see that this 14 year old Chicana was infinitely more qualified to lead society than the u.s. vice-president. She doesn't need the Dan Quayles (or their women) to"protect" her. She and others simply need power over their own lives.

World capitalism maintains thousands of organizations and institutions to regulate and repress its human property, ranging from the so-called Right to Life movement to the departments of children and family services, all the way up to the United Nations Children's Fund (UNICEF), the u.n. agency supposedly"protecting" the world's children.

UNICEF's real mission is to promote favorable conditions for child slave and semi-slave labor for capitalism in the Third World. Which is why it was no surprise that in 1987 the president of the UNICEF committee in Belgium was forced to resign after it was revealed that the men in his group, including the 63 year-old director, Jos Verbeeck, were running an international child pornography business in UNICEF's Brussel's headquarters. Children were used in sex, photographed and videoed, by what police described as "a major child sex ring" operating out of UNICEF.[83]

That same year, 1987, by no coincidence, UNICEF published a glossy book detailing *The State of the World's Children*, 1987. There was not so much as one word on the millions of child slave and semi-slave laborers. Not one slave-owner was named, not one major u.s. corporation was exposed, not one slave-master nation was named. It was all whited-out.*

Instead, UNICEF emphasized its mass health projects, like vaccination campaigns and oral rehydration therapy for diarrhea. These inexpensive projects are saving the lives of millions of Third World children who might otherwise die too soon to swell capitalism's giant labor pool of surplus Third World children. This is why capitalism has UNICEF—not to "protect" children but as part of its world personnel department.

While the *false ideology of work* implanted in our consciousness keeps us thinking that child labor, like women's labor, is secondary and marginal, it is a basic necessity to capitalism as a system. Just as slavery is. Since 1950 the labor pool of child workers and potential workers has more than doubled, cresting over 1.1 billion between the ages of 5–14 years old in 1987.[84] In 1986 the International Labor Organization (ILO) estimated that there were *88 million children employed in the world labor force*. In that figure the ILO did *not* include any children under age 11, children doing piecework at home, or those "informally" employed as farm workers, street peddlers, garbage scavengers, criminals,

---

* By 1991, UNICEF'S annual *State of the World's Children* report finally spent a page admitting children were exploited as semi-slave labor, but said that they were "helpless" to do anything about it. Again, no corporations, religions, or governments were named.

and prostitutes. If all those child workers were included, a UNICEF staff paper admitted, "the estimate would run into the hundreds of millions."

"Hundreds of millions." Capitalism's false ideology of work keeps telling us that adult male workers in major nations are what's really important, while child labor is an economically unimportant fringe activity. However, it turns out that a continental industrial power like the u.s.a. has under 165,000 adult male steelworkers—while there are "hundreds of millions" of child laborers in the Third World.

We can see why this world class structure is so hidden. Let's go back to the scene of the crime, to Macy's—and Hiyat. For weaving that five square yard rug for Macy's, 11 year-old Hiyat received about $19.34 from her adult bosses at Mocary SA. That represents almost three weeks of labor for her. They in turn sold the rug to Macy's in Manhattan for $166.40, keeping, quite obviously, a healthy little profit for themselves. Macy's then paid shipping companies, insurance companies, and u.s. customs duties for that rug of $50.84, for a total cost to them of $217.24. Macy's then added their own markup of well over 100% to get a final retail "sale" price of $499.

What must be kept off screen is this entire class structure in which the Hiyats and the Afrikan workers in Soweto, the Caribbean women making N.B.A. basketballs, blouses and a myriad of other u.s. products, the homeless agricultural laborers in Chile stocking u.s. supermarkets, are the source of the great wealth of the metropolis. It is their unseen lives that are stolen to sustain the neo-imperial civilization. Just as the often told glories of Imperial Rome were but a shell, an artifice of parasitism over the life labors of uncounted millions of their slave laborers.

As we bring into light this class structure, the category of Hiyat's child labor merges into that of women's labor. In the same way, the "veiled slavery" of semi-slave wage labor clearly is close to "slavery pure and simple," is really part of the same process. And what we think of as the crisis of oppressed Third World nations rises up most sharply as the crisis of an oppressed gender. Because all these separate categories are but sides of the hidden life of *one* class, the postmodern industrial proletariat. Which is today emerging as the most important class in the world.

To triangulate the path of the shockwave that is reorganizing everything around us, we need to go back to the periphery, to the oppressed world and the class changes taking place there.

Capitalism's need to proletarianize women and children on a world scale is by its very nature a vast human enterprise. Once, after all, to exploit North Amerika, to conquer the Indian Nations and stand guard over millions of Afrikan slave laborers, required a counterweight of millions and then tens of millions of people loyal to euro-capitalism. This class counterweight took the form of an artificial white race and a white settler nation. To exploit and hold down hundreds of millions of women and children workers spread over a hundred and fifty countries, transnational capitalism requires an even larger counterweight. And now, what is class is cast in the form of gender and disguised as "natural." The counterweight is male society.

MACHO NATIONALISM & FINANCE CAPITAL

The blindspot in middle-class white feminism is that it always breaks short of bringing the feminist spotlight of theoretical analysis home, of completing it. Undercovering the secret relationship between the transformation in Third World women's condition and the transformation in their own. With that gap, the misimpression is left that white women in amerikkka have the same gender relationship to capitalism that Third World women do, supposedly differing only in degree by being a bit less oppressed.

In this relationship, finance capital is the chain—not merely between nations or between rich vs. poor—between women of the periphery and women of the metropolis. Finance capital has a lot to do, it turns out, with transformation of gender today.

What may be hard to see at home, close up, jumps into our eyes when we stand back and view the entire neo-colonial empire. Brazil is an example of the new industrialization of the Third World (we could have chosen South Afrika or China or the Persian Gulf, as well). What is so striking compared to the colonial past is the development of macho industries once monopolized by the metropolis.

Armored cars, armored personnel carriers and tanks for capitalist armies used to be exports from FMC or Cadillac-Gage in the u.s. or Vickers in England. Today, the Engesa company in Brazil is the largest exporter in the West of such military vehicles. Its export sales in 1985 were $600 million. Over 5,000 Brazilian Engesa armored cars and troop carriers are in use by the armies of Chile, Saudi Arabia, Iran, Egypt, Iraq, the People's Republic of China, and other nations. "We now produce 50 percent of all wheeled military vehicles made in the Free World today," Jose Luiz Whitalcer Ribeiro, the owner of Englesa, has boasted.[85]

Brazil is the fifth largest arms exporter (and has the eighth-largest industrial economy) in the world. Its inexpensive Tauras handguns, from pocket deuce-deuces to copies of the 9mm beretta, sell well in white gunshops, while Britain's Royal Air Force purchased 130 Brazilian Tucano jet trainers. The Brazilian arms industry at its peak in the 1980s employed over 100,000 workers, producing simple, less expensive military hardware for mostly Third World armies.

Obviously, a nation that can design and manufacture its own missiles, machine guns, tanks and jets is no longer underdeveloped in the old colonial sense. Yet, transnational capitalism and the u.s. remain serenely unworried about this emerging industrial "competition." The u.s. government has even encouraged and aided Brazil's arms industry—and Brazilian export sales in general. Over protests from u.s. suppliers and rivals, Washington approved the sales to u.s. commuter airlines of the Brazilian Bandeirante turboprop passenger plane, as well as the regular flow of Brazilian oranges for Minutemaid and other u.s. frozen juice corporations. Appeals from Kansas aircraft manufacturers, Connecticut arms makers, and Florida growers were ignored by Federal regulators and trade officials.

The simple reason is that these Brazilian corporations, while certainly enriching Brazil's small capitalist class, are even more profitable than u.s. corporations are for Western finance capital. The $1 billion a year that Brazil earned during the 1980s exporting arms only made a connecting flight to Brazil before homing to its true owners in New York and London, Zurich and Bonn. Brazil, which was indebted to the Western banks to the tune of $104 billion at last count, during the 1980s was sending them 5% of its gross national product each year (equivalent to 23% of all its domestic savings) just to make the *interest* payments.[86] The "debt crisis" was merely the breakdown of Brazil's economy and society under the intolerable burden.

In the colonial era, the white metropolis held a tight monopoly on industrialization and technology. Now, in the neo-colonial empire, finance capital encourages industry in the Third World up to and including nuclear technology, because the profits from this industrialization simply flow back to them as debt repayments.

Under this reign of finance capital, the u.s. has become not only parasitic but a usurer society, caring mainly that the nations of the oppressed world remain its debt slaves, perpetually laboring without payment. Transnational capitalism cares about its exports of products to the Third World (now 35% of all u.s. exports and rising), but even more important is the export of capital.

While a popular racism is maintained that the oppressed world is the net receiver of billions and billions of dollars from the metropolis in the form of "aid" and easy credit, the stark truth is that they are net *givers*. Each year they are as a whole *poorer*, sending amerikkka more goods and dollars than they have received. The more a Brazil or a Mexico industrializes, the poorer the majority of its people are. This is why these nations are debt slaves to the empire of a new type. A 1988 report on the "debt crisis" revealed:

> "... Lending to Latin America has in fact been phenomenally profitable for most banks and syndicators, yielding returns on equity of 50 percent or more per year. In fact, if we treat any interests

above ordinary profit rates as a return on principal,
our banks have already been more fully paid back
by the countries ...

"In retrospect this has not been cheap. From 1983
to 1988, for example, Mexico forked over about
$33 billion in interest to its foreign creditors, while
receiving back only $13 billion in net new foreign
loans ... In Mexico itself, the distribution of this
debt burden has been extremely inequitable. First,
there are few productive assets to show for all the
debts ... Many Mexicans now actually have lower
per capita incomes than in the early 1970s, before
the borrowing spree began."

What finance capital does is really loan sharking. Oppressed
nations find that they're paying the u.s. banks back two or
three times what they've borrowed—and still owe the "principal" or original debt. Like the crack dealer who "loans" his
addict-customer $5 in dope but demands $10 repayment the
next day. The dealer isn't doing anything that the big bankers aren't doing, only the later are sharking entire nations.

Brazil, the neo-colony of this new empire, is in crucial ways un-developing as a coherent society the more it
becomes an industrial hell. In the poverty-stricken rural
Northeast, 1987 saw the first outbreak of bubonic plague,
the dreaded Black Death that claimed tens of millions of
lives in Europe's Middle Ages. Another medieval disease,
leprosy, has also grown to epidemic levels in Brazil, with
more than 250,000 leprosy victims. "We are seeing a general
deterioration," said Dr. Delosmar Mendonca, public health
official in Joao Pessoa. Records kept at the University of
Recife prove that because of "chronic malnutrition" children

in the 1980s were being born with smaller heads and less development than before. "We are moving toward a generation of dwarfs," Dr. Mendonca said.[87]

Neo-colonialism is not the end of colonialism, then, but its continuation on a higher level of world development; literally meaning a *"new and different" colonialism*. In the same way, the industrial proletariat whose core is women and children has from its origins centuries ago always been a *colonized* class and this is even more true now that it has become a world class. A class that is colonized not by gender alone, but by the fusion of race and nation as well.

In her provocative book, *Bananas, Beaches and Bases: Making Feminist Sense of International Politics*, Cynthia Enloe points out how the new wave of capitalist industrialization of the Third World takes the form of gender-specific industries which are only "traditional" to euro-capitalism. There is *macho industry* ("heavy industry"), such as aviation, steel, chemicals, shipbuilding, arms, as well as government civil service and the mercenary military, which employ men.

And then there is *feminine industry* ("light industry"), such as textiles, electronics, garments, shoemaking, agricultural harvesting, food processing, tourism, consumer goods, and data entry (u.s. banks and insurance companies have their data put on magnetic tape everywhere from Beijing to Ireland to the Dominican Republic), which employ mostly women and children.

Macho industry employs fewer workers and is often unprofitable—being capital intensive it requires those massive billions in Western bank loans—but is nevertheless said to be the most important for new patriarchal nations and pays the highest wages. Much of it, including the mercenary military and police, the State bureaucracy, and "prestige" industries like aviation and shipbuilding, are non-productive in terms of the needs of society. The most important effect of macho industry, however, is to subsidize stratas and classes of men to be the owners of women.

Feminine industry employs most workers and is the main source of both profit and socially necessary goods, but pays far less, of course. By giving industry a gender—as *they once gave slave agriculture a race*—capitalism can throw a veil over the extreme exploitation and semi-slavery of its women and children workers. Cynthia Enloe comments:

> "Organizing factory jobs, designing machinery and factory rules to keep women productive and feminine—these were crucial strategies in Europe's industrial growth. Industrialized textile production and garment-making were central to Britain's global power. Both industries feminized labor in order to make it profitable and internationally competitive. Other countries learned the British lesson in order to compete in the emerging global political economy and to stave off foreign control.

> "The making of the 'mill girl' proved crucial. American textile investors travelled from Boston to England to learn the formula in the early decades of the nineteenth century. Japanese entrepreneurs, backed by their government's Meiji reforms to resist Western colonization, also chose young rural women as their first industrial workers. In industrializing Tsarist Russia, owners of new textile factories steadily increased the proportion of women workers, with government approval. In the pre-World War I period gendered formulas

for factory-fueled capitalism seemed to be traded
as energetically as railroad stocks. Neither war nor
revolution has done much to transform the femi-
nizing strategies used by both capitalist and socialist garment-factory managers."[88]

**To paraphrase Marx, the veiled slavery of women and chil-
dren wage workers in the new industrial zones requires
as its pedestal the naked slavery of women as the social
property of men.** While Enloe's insights into devaluing
women's work can be misread as being about mere discrimination, the root of this devaluation is that no slave-owning
society expects its slaves to have real income of their own.

The majority of the productive work done by the human
race is, in fact, *unwaged labor* performed under duress by
women and children. Not only raising crops and providing
cooking, laundry, cleaning and sexual services to men, but in
maintaining a community and reproducing physically and
socially the next generation of workers, women's *unwaged
labor* is such an absolute necessity to male society that it is
considered part of Nature along with forests and oceans and
rainfall. The rightful bounty of men to share or fight over.
All *waged* labor rests upon the greater foundation of wom-
en's *unwaged* labor. This is why outlines of class structure
based solely upon *waged labor* aren't accurate. No more than
they would have been in the Old Slave South.

Cynthia Enloe points out:

"As South Korean government officials were bid-
ding to have their country chosen as the site of the
1988 Olympics, some commentators were talking
about the 'two Koreas'. They didn't mean North

and South. They were referring to the South Korea
of large, capitalized heavy industries and the South
Korea of the back-alley garment workshop. *In 1988
women made up an estimated two-thirds of workers in
South Korea's world famous export-oriented factories.*
They were working more hours per week than their
male counterparts and being paid on average one
third less, producing clothes, electronics, shoes
and data services—industries that enabled South
Korean businessmen to accumulate enough capital to launch their own companies. Those Korean
women factory workers who went on strike in the
1980s to bring down the authoritarian military
government were protesting against both the myth
of the successful South Korea and the price that
South Korean factory women were expected to pay
to sustain that myth."[89]

Keying back to "Blade Runner": one of the underlying truths
in the movie's subtext is that capitalism does raise up whole
new classes to meet its economic needs by making new races
and genders. But also, when these classes become obsolete
to its needs or too dangerous—threatening slave rebellions—capitalism is prepared not only to repress them, but
to transform or even eliminate them in their millions. This
is the battleground of our time and place.

Toppled by -isms

White males say they're now the minority it's OK to oppress

By Joyce Price
THE WASHINGTON TIMES

Some white men say they make up one of the most maligned minorities in the United States.

They're victims, they say, of racism and sexism and have little recourse to redress wrongs against them.

Their once-definitive influence on American society is ebbing amid a tide of intolerance, and, if several demographic studies are correct, they're a vanishing breed of American.

"There's heavy discriminati[on] against white males," says Fr[ed] Bertels, founder and director of [a] Miami-based Male Liberation Fo[un]dation. "They are losing job pro[mo]tions because affirmative ac[tion] doesn't give them the proper pro[mo]tion benefits they deserve."

Fredric Hayward, executive [di]rector of the California-based M[en's] Rights advocacy group, puts it [this] way: "I hear a lot of white men [com]plain. They aren't saying the[y de]serve to be privileged. I hear t[hem] complain that now that we've raised consciousness about sexism and racism, both of which are wrong, that they are now the victims of it."

Affirmative action "is just a euphemism for discrimination," Mr. Hayward says. "There is no valid excuse for discrimination. ... It's wrong."

Across the nation, psychiatrists, psychologists, union chiefs and leaders of men's rights groups are hearing the same kinds of complaints from white men these days.

Historically the holders of the major share of power and money in

see MEN, *page A12*

ONE HOUR PARKING 9 A.M 6 P.M SUN

TOW AWAY ZONE NO STANDING

YOUR STANDARD OF LIVING SOMETIMES DEMANDS THE EXPLOITATION OF PEOPLE AND NATURE

LOSING GROUND
A survey of 311 men found they think th[ey] are losing ground. Percentage of white m[en who] feel:

■ They are losing an advantage in terms of [jobs a]nd incomes: 56%

■ They are losing influence in American so[ciety:] 4[8]%

CHAPTER SEVEN:

THE CHANGER
AND THE CHANGED

*"The weapon of criticism cannot replace
the criticism of weapons."*—the Moor

Cut to the chase: What does this mean to us in practice?
What's different in terms of political strategy & tactics, different in the terrain of struggle? We can begin by outlining
first understandings. The previous capitalist world order
was bipolar, with everyone visible massed around opposing poles of oppressor vs. oppressed. It was colonized vs.
colonizer, white vs. black, invader vs. indigenous. **But at
its essence, the growing chaos of the neo-colonial world
order is that many different peoples—armed with conflicting capitalist agendas—have been loosed to fight it
out.** As transnational capitalism hides behind & backs first
one side and then the other—or both—to indirectly use the
chaos they see no class interest in containing.

This chaos is itself a deepening contradiction of the
system, one that no one can be certain of riding, not even
the ruling class. And on this charged terrain, dis-unity and
not unity is the changed strategic need of the oppressed.
This is hard to grab, since it goes against truisms inherited
from colonial times. And we think that dis-unity is what's
spontaneously going on all around us anyway, when it's
really an unconscious unity around wrong principles. Old

slogans used the picture of unity to make people feel strong: "Sisterhood Is Powerful"; "Black Unity"; "The People United Will Never Be Defeated." But these are dead phrases now, not truths but decaying shells.

Racial & gender & nation politics can't take the form they did across the river back in the old days, in segregated Montgomery, Ala. in 1955 or even pent-up Harlem in 1965. Look closely at the folding contradictions, the living process in all things that drives the coming into being of the new & the waning of the old.

Capitalism absolutely owns the social system, but no longer finds it in its class interest to totally control or regulate every single space. And perhaps couldn't even if it exerted itself to. This is where our accurate sense of growing chaos comes from.

In the colonial era everything was relatively rigid, over-controlled, characterized by an insistence on euro-patriarchal order. New Afrikans, for example, were not only limited in what jobs they could have, where and how they could live, but were constrained to act towards europeans by rules demanding deference and acted-out inferiority. Like white women act towards white men. Now contrast the 1954 lynching of teenager Emmett Till in Mississippi for supposedly being disrespectful towards a white woman to rapper Ice-T in neo-colonial 1992, who after coming out with a song mock-threatening to rape a 12 year-old white girl, was able to buy himself a $1.2 million mansion on the Sunset Strip.

It isn't that there aren't plenty of white people who'd like to lynch Ice-T, but it's also true that big business itself is grooming and promoting Ice-T's verbal masturbation act. (and millions of young males, white and Black, are buying the same macho music as though Dick is now their race).

The controversy over Ice-T's pathetic little cop-killing

rap only highlights how our political struggles are no longer simply bipolar. It isn't as simple as Black vs. White any more. The good side vs. the bad side. There's many more players and agendas in the game, whether it's Black Genocide or the break-up of whiteoslavia you're dealing with. The physics of political struggle has new rules.

Take the Ice-T censorship controversy: on the Ice-T side you had not only Black musicians and artists, teenagers of all races, Jewish record company executives and the giant Time Warner corporation, but also gay white civil libertarians and Afro-centric muslim activists. "It's a big country and some-one's got to furnish it."

On the "gag him" side you had the masses of police, both presidential campaigns, christian churches, and most white settler opinion over age 30 (many white kids were for Ice-T, since as long as he's only postmodern blackface, only enter-taining them, what dif does it make?) Wasn't a multicultural capitalism backing and using both sides, even though they had clashing agendas?

Trans-national capitalism is driving a certain kind of breakthrough idea, a "multicultural" worldview in which each people and grouping is freed and encouraged to explore its own capitalist agenda no matter what form it takes. From Slavic Holy Russian anti-semitism to lesbian small busi-nesses. The Cuban takeover in Miami is as mellow to Time Warner, Sony and Citibank as Afro-hip-hop stars making millions selling CD's damning whites as "devils."

Even when whole nations teeter on the brink of auto-genocide in made-up capitalistic gang-wars—as is happen-ing in Black Somalia or White Yugoslavia this year—it's chill. Everyone is free to go for it, free to fight it out any way they want so long as they don't endanger the system itself. No one is protected, either, of course.

This is not a strategy, but an inescapable consequence of changes in basic production & distribution. The imperialism of the multinational corporations is trying to untangle itself from the outgrown shell of its early national form. Starting to distance itself from, while still utilizing, the very nations and races and genders it grew out of. After all, the faded glories of the British empire and its "Anglo-Saxon civilization" are zero help to outmoded British corporations fighting to survive. No more help, really, than Harvard, the AFL-CIO, and the "American Way of Life" was to General Motors when it was being beaten up in the alley by Honda, Toyota and Mercedes-Benz.

Nations per se are less useful to the imperialism of the multinationals, just as dialectically they become even more vital to everyone else, from emerging capitalist cliques to outlaw communities of the oppressed (since you aren't going to have any say in the shifting transnational economy going on above you, it becomes even more important to have some territory or space of your own).

It isn't any outside force, but capitalism itself that is destabilizing white amerikkka. That's why the far rightwing, who in the past worked with the government and saw themselves as the domestic defenders of amerikkkanism, have given up on this nation, and now call for overthrowing the u.s. government (which they label "ZOG" or zionist occupation government) in Civil War 2. They've admitted that the u.s. is already too mix and match to ever be anglo-saxon again, and want to take the five paler states of the Northwest and build their own Aryan nation. So the armed white right spends much more emotion and bullets fighting the IRS, federal marshals, ATF and other government agencies than it does the Black community.

DE-SETTLERIZING THE "U.S.A.": CRISES AT THE CENTER

White men are so bone-hostile to multiculturalism not because of their racism or sexism alone, but because they sense that it foreshadows their own demise as a nation. This evolution of amerikkka takes the form of de-settlerization. The u.s.a., historically powered-up as a european men's settler empire of invaders and occupiers, is being pushed by capitalism to give way to a more cosmopolitan and post-modern society even against die-harder resistance of the white majority. The current trend of multi culturalism being picked up by capitalist institutions—from legitimizing the Gay community to emphasizing the art and literature of Indians, New Afrikans, Asians & Latinos—is the surface reflection of capitalism's de-settlerization away from the dead white men's society.

The material facts of economic production & class rule are the basis of every historic change, and nowhere is this more evident than in restructuring postmodern amerikkka, where races and genders are now being erased and rewritten over like software. Our own political-military understanding must keep up with the transformation, and grasp what is the root of change.

The imperialism of the multinational corporations no longer needs either the white settler nation or the once-colonized but still intractable New Afrikan nation. It needs many of their people, particularly white women and Black women for its economy, but not their entire nations, and certainly not in their previous forms. It's just the bottom line. Both are populations that are in *different* ways too expensive and politically too untrustworthy from the ruling class perspective.

As we can see all around us, a new multicultural labor force is being imported by the tens of millions to take up the slack. You don't have to be Einstein to catch on that the media are selling an image that imported Asians and Latinos are "good" citizens, with a work ethic and modest wage demands, while both whites & New Afrikans are criticized as lazy and greedy in comparison—or worse, in the case of New Afrikans. In a recent issue of the *Atlantic* magazine, Jack Miles of the *Los Angeles Times* staff writes of how:

> "Latinos, even when they are foreign, seem native
> and safe, while Blacks, who are native, seem foreign
> and dangerous. In saying this, I am saying some-
> thing that I shrink from saying and grieve to say,
> but I think it's true."[90]

Now the historic New Afrikan "inner city" is being increasingly depopulated, scattering Black communities to both prisons and a spread of outlying small towns. Which are a new system of reservations, outside the real economy and society, where New Afrikans of the "dangerous class" can be penned up—not for labor but for gradual elimination. While there is still no answer for capitalism's family contradiction of what to do with the excess millions of useless white men they subsidize both here and in europe.

This crisis at their own center comes dialectically out of their triumph. Out of world domination, a super-parasitism developed that made euro-amerikans, and especially white men, the least productive and most highly subsidized people since the fall of Rome. Even world looting by capitalism can no longer afford to keep subsidizing close to 200 million euro-amerikans in the old way.

White reformers may dream of a Scandinavian-style

welfare state, but the u.s. already has a welfare state: a settler welfare state oriented not toward social services but toward subsiding high white individual income. This has been the basis of the whole culture. Government welfare is actually centered on the white middle class. Half of all u.s. households have some member receiving government subsidy.[91] Thirty per cent of the total u.s. population directly receives government cash or cash-equivalent aid in some form (VA Benefits, Medicare, Social Security, Food Stamps, etc.), but when we add in disguised welfare in the form of tax benefits, it turns out that the average white household with an income of over $100,000 received $9,280 in government subsidy in 1991.[92]

Contrary to the self-serving assumption that Welfare primarily goes to Black and Latino poor, government subsidy is centered on the upper layers of the white population. Even two-thirds of all Medicare funds are estimated to go to the white middle-class. Over $400 billion was distributed in 1991 by the federal government to households with over $30,000 incomes. Nor does this include hidden subsidies such as non-productive government employment (in October 1991, for the first time, the number of people employed by the government was greater than those employed in all u.s. manufacturing).[93]

There are thousands of different ways that white business has been subsidized, from the huge Exxon corporation being allowed to not pay corporate income tax down to the anachronistic and largely unknown system of farm supports. Honeybee farmers receive an extra 100% of their crops' value every year, for example, while sugar beet farmers get an annual average of $100,000 each from Washington. No subsidy for white people was too outrageous to be considered.[94]

Once the protected monopoly markets of the colonial

period vanished, capitalism could no longer afford Michigan autoworkers who make $32 an hour in wages and benefits or construction workers who made almost as much. To say nothing of useless layers of "suits" who just pass faxes back and forth to each other. Capitalism is now cracking down, throwing excess yuppies out of the lifeboat and demanding that white workers start to live low like workers, not like professionals or minor members of the British aristocracy.

What's intensifying the contradiction tearing settler-ism apart is that most white people left production behind them, and no longer expect to do the hard, basic work of society. Here is hubris, the arrogant demands of a master race pushing itself over the edge. It's typical in this culture that cowboys are "in" now among whites. From "Young Guns" on television to Clint Eastwood's old-fart western, "The Unforgiven." Cowboy hats are common gear for macho men, while women in Greenwich Village wear cowgirl boots or their look-alikes. Props for a poser culture. But "Nobody wants to be a cowboy," observes Oracia Mercado of the Mountain Plains Agricultural Service, which arranges the importation of Mexican ranch-hands for Wyoming farms. "It's hard work, it's dirty work, it's year-round work. It's not something a U.S. worker wants to do."

Even in Wyoming, where white unemployment is so high small towns are closing down, young whites are no longer willing to take these jobs. Nor are they willing to live the hard, isolated life of sheep herders or sheep shearers (sea-sonal specialists who come in to cut the wool off sheep). Sheepherders in the West are no longer euro-amerikans, coming instead from Mexico and the Basque in Spain, Chile and Australia. The shortage of workers for this lonely job is so great that the u.s. government has issued work permits for Mongolian herders now flown in by the farmers associations. White people only want to start as ranch owners or maybe marketing executives. That's entry-level to them.

Niche by niche the real class structure is being transformed and fought over in the neo-colonial changeover. At expensive Washington, d.c. restaurants the busboys and dishwashers are no longer Black but Salvadorans. On the Mall, the long rows of vending trailers selling tourists everything from Georgetown sweatshirts to hot dogs are not owned by white men but Koreans. In the white suburbs, the real estate salespersons are increasingly white women. Cubans dominate the gas station business in Miami, just as Asian Indians control the newspaper stands in New York City and the cheap motels in the Deep South (as in the film "Mississippi Masala"). Just as women and Asians are making inroads in scientific higher education.

When Xerox corporation needed a saviour to fight back the gains made by copier rivals Kodak and Canon, they made the best marketing executive they could find their Executive Vice-President—even though he is an Afrikan-Amerikan man. Atlanta's Coca-Cola corporation found they needed a Spanish chief executive to lead their world-wide comeback in the 1980s against Pepsi, in the same way that a culturally Southern-white Pentagon had to turn to General Colin Powell to rebuild itself.

The number of capitalist niches reserved for white men keep shrinking, step by step, just as the u.s. economy and wage levels seem to be permanently falling into an unknown 21st century. White men are really confused, like a gunman who keeps clicking the trigger not believing his gun is on empty. But they aren't going to give up, because they can't.

CONFLICTS DON'T NEED RESOLUTIONS

De-settlerization is a process already in motion, but its completion is not a given, not a certainty, any more than Civil Rights or Roe v. Wade. What is a done deal is that multinational capitalism is de-settlerizing its own institutions—not only corporations, but foundations, universities—in a global way, taking advantage of new talent while making a necessary show of how unprejudiced they are (which is why the Ford Foundation has an Afrikan-Amerikan president and Ford dealers advertise in Gay community newspapers). But other than that, capitalism is letting the ants fight it out.

The fundamental crisis about nations today extends right into the future of the u.s.a. White men are up in arms and they're right, of course. Neo-colonialism isn't just "nice to Negroes week" and fronting off with a Puerto Rican politician or two—it's everything. From who gets the job to who gets the woman to who gets to be a real person. The whole ball game. For things that Colonialism shaped are coming undone.

White men and their loyal women have no intention of surrendering their nation, and are counter-attacking. So Fords and Rockefellers may fund Planned Parenthood and the government may enact Roe v. Wade, but abortion clinics are being harassed and firebombed out of business in a spreading pattern in county after county, state after state. White settlers make their own laws, after all. They don't care what the Supremes sing.

Women construction workers are now officially "welcome" by the white boy's unions and contractors, but mysteriously always get laid off the day before they're eligible to join the union, get harassed out or never get hired. Especially Black women and Asian women & Latinas. The media gives the mis-impression that this is solely due to redneck construction workers or backward "ethnic" Catholic unions, when it's simply amerikkkan to reserve the best for white men.

For example, Arnold Diaz of WCBS exposed Tischman Construction (the largest Jewish developer-contractor in New York City) for hiring 0% women workers in both the new Mt. Sinai Hospital building and in the federally-subsidized new wing for Rockefeller University. That's 0%, as in not one, not any. Pure Dick. When questioned, a spokesperson for Tischman said that hiring men only was approved by Rockefeller's equal opportunity staff: "They've reviewed our record and they're satisfied."[95]

This Fall a mob of 5,000 New York City police took over the City Hall grounds in protest against Mayor Uncle Thomas and his plan for a civilian review board. Drunk cops harassed and threatened an Afrikan-Amerikan city councilwoman trying to get into City Hall, derisively calling her "nigger woman" in front of reporters. Mayor Uncle Tom, as all the guys on the street know, may be just a clothing store dummy picked by the white power structure, but that's not settleristic enough for white people. Today's Black genocide in the indirect neo-colonial way isn't fast enough to satisfy the euro-amerikan grass roots, who remember that the first lesson of their "Americanism" is "The only good Indian is a dead Indian."

No one wants to say it, but if Civil Rights were ever put to a "democratic" white vote (the concepts "democratic" and "white" are mutually contradictory to each other) it would lose hands-down. All these neo-colonial reforms have been imposed on the white garrison society from above, and they hate it as the horse hates the bit in his mouth.

Diane Sawyer from CBS News was probing the unfairness of "community service" probation sentences. She showed videos of young Black and Latin men doing their court-ordered "community service" by unpaid heavy construction labor, while noting that wealthy white men like Reagan aides John Deaver and Ollie North are assigned farcical non-jobs like giving talks at drug abuse clinics. Sawyer then interviewed a prominent California lawyer who specializes in "fixing" these cases. This is what he was unafraid to say on national television:

> Sawyer: "Shouldn't we have the Norths, the Deavers, breaking bricks just like the Black inner city men who sell drugs?"
>
> Lawyer: (breaks into laughter) "We can sit around and say that. That's nice to say, but it'll never happen."
>
> Sawyer: "Why?"
>
> Lawyer: "Because we aren't going to punish our own—as white people who run this country."[96]

ARMIES ALREADY IN MOTION

This isn't something that capitalism can change by simply pushing a button. Any more than they can just order capitalistic men with AK-47s to stop slaughtering to set up their cherished tribal nations in Cambodia or Croatia or Liberia. Because capitalism in its struggle to control the entire world set armies in motion. And these armies, which take the form of entire nations and races and genders, are still out on a mission from colonial days. Just as capitalism created white patriarchal society to be its settler garrison over North Amerika, and after 400 years this has a historic momentum and a stubborn life of its own. Clinton or Rockefeller can't just make a phone call and get 200 millions of white men and their women to roll over and pull the plug, to stop being parasites. All over the world armies long set in motion refuse to be recalled.

Which is why white men aren't going to ever give up attacking women. They were empowered by capitalism long ago to own women, and they aren't going to non-violently give it up. The war over who controls women's bodies isn't about values or babies, it's all about which classes live or die. Multinational capitalism freed white women from being breeders, encouraged them to crash the good jobs and start careers and own property of their own. Contrary to our self-delusions, white women didn't win any of this. In the 1960s there were no mass feminist urban riots, no white women with molotov cocktails saying "burn, baby, burn!", no mass civil disobedience by white women jamming the jails, no militant armed organization of white women, no nothing. The box of goodies came from Great White Father.

Capitalism itself got the idea for this neo-colonial

"equality" because it no longer wanted white women to stay home and reproduce larger numbers of even more non-productive white people demanding to be subsidized. That's the last thing capitalism needs. And on the other hand, that's why the right wing wants to force women back to the patriarchal bedroom, to jumpstart white demographics and keep this continent a white-majority nation. They say so, too, that their "Western Civilization" is dependent on car-bombing Roe v. Wade and forcing white women back to reproduce overtime. So in the struggle over the ownership of women's bodies, a number of sides, with not just gender politics but class agendas and nation agendas and race agendas, are freely battling it out with no end in sight.

And in this chaos, we can do much more than we thought we could. Sliding around government pre-occupation with "more important" crises, moving and hiding amidst the chaotic clash of different players, the oppressed learned that in the physics of this new political universe we really can do much more than we thought we could—while others, don't forget, can do the same to us.

We know of a small neighborhood where feminists were angry at a porn shop being open right on the main business street, where women had to shop. Many women, responding to a leaflet, began telephoning the porn business to democratically tell them to get out—oh, incidentally tying up their phone and clerk. So the porn store changed to an unlisted number and pulled its ad out of the Yellow Pages.

Then, one morning, the neighborhood woke up to find the porn store burned out, its broken windows covered with plywood sheets (on which some persons had sprayed, "STOP PORNOGRAPHY"). If Amazons did do it, they didn't issue a press statement identifying themselves or a political communiqué daring the f.b.i. to hunt them out. "The action is the communique." Actually, anyone might have done it these days, not just Amazons. Maybe those religious rightwingers who also are against porn shops did it. Maybe the store was arsoned to collect insurance money, by the Syndicate. Do you think the government is going to sort all this out or bother to protect all those little porn shops? Not hardly. Of course, many months later, after things had cooled, the porn shop re-opened with a blank front of cinderblock and steel, no window display or signs, no sight of the interior and a locked steel door you have to get buzzed through after being checked out. Dick zips it up. The struggle continues, act 2 ...

This new political physics is at work in all social dimensions. Technically illegal but tolerated survival economics, for example, have always gone on in the New Afrikan community, from unlicensed after hours clubs to informal street vending. The ruling class tolerated it because they knew it was in their interests, too, since their labor pool had to survive somehow (and most white settlers didn't care what went on "over there"). Now, that integration has come, many official Afrikan-Amerikan leaders are complaining that Black economics isn't succeeding because they aren't being subsidised like white people are, and they insist New Afrikan people need more high-class welfare ("minority set-asides" and the rest) from the government.

While these neo-colonial beggars in three-piece suits are whining, other unfamous and ordinary working Afrikans are just doing it—and nibbling away at government functions, too. If you stand at a corner along Flatbush avenue in Brooklyn during the day, every couple of minutes an Afrikan-owned gypsy van comes by to take Afro-commuters into downtown Brooklyn and Manhattan. Unlicensed, semi-illegal, charging only $1 to the MTA's $1.25 fare for the B41 bus or subway, the hundreds of Afrikan-owned vans on Flatbush alone are an unpublicized Afro-transit system competing successfully with the subsidized euro-government transit system in the heart of the metropolis. The Montgomery Bus Boycott in 1955 was a world sensation, but this is going on unnoticed under the snow.

While it's mostly Afrikan-Caribbean immigrants who do vans on Flatbush and Afrikan guys from the Sudan who drive the livery cars (unlicensed taxi services) in that area, there are unlicensed vans, buses and cars providing public transit in all boroughs of New York City and out on Long Island. Run by whites, also, as well as a dozen other nationalities. The NYPD office of Management Analysis and Planning says that their euro-transit system is losing "Nearly $1 million a day" from illegal carriers. Some MTA bus routes have admittedly lost more than 15% of their riders to Afro-transit.[97]

The MTA has "fear of the Black Planet," and has its transit cops coming up out of the subway to issue thousands of summons to Afro-transit vans, hoping to harass them out of business. It's not even a question whether the euro-government could shut it all down. Militarily speaking, the NYPD could do it in one day, to say nothing of the 1st Armored Division. But politically speaking, at a time when capitalism isn't even pretending to stop drug sales, muggings and burglaries, to do Operation Desert Storm on Black working people providing a needed human service, would raise consciousness too much.

So both sides are maneuvering, with the police writing tickets and trying to harass it back underground. Maybe tomorrow they'll make a big move and maybe no, in the neo-colonial environment where power, borders and laws have no exact lines. Afro-transit has created itself just as Hip-Hop did, probing the limits day-to-day. This is no big deal, just a small example from daily life. It is the indeterminate environment the oppressed learn to take advantage of, sink or swim. In this chaos, we can do much more than we thought we could, just as others can do it to us.

MULTICULTURALISM WON'T SAVE YOUR LIFE

Nowadays, there are a lot of hopeful illusions going around about multiculturalism; hopeful but definitely not harmless. Illusions that are helping to determine life or death. Nor are these postmodernist illusions any accident. People deliberately misunderstand multiculturalism—if only subconsciously—because of the attractive pull at the core of capitalist culture, which is parasitism. This is the question we've been heading for all along.

We've been caught off guard by it, but in the neo-colonial transition the culture of parasitism that used to be characteristic primarily of euro-patriarchal society has hopped all kinds of dividing lines, and has now spread deeply into other races, nations, and genders. Materially, this is because parasitism itself is an extreme factor of class, while neo-colonialism has recast social relationships by raising up new capitalistic subcultures, stratas and classes in the formerly colonized. Blurring and mixing up old dividing lines.

Cross-over culture at work.

Vincent Chin had never heard of multiculturalism or neo-colonialism before a white man beat him to death with a baseball bat outside a Burger King in Detroit. But that's what he died from. Chin, a 27 year-old Chinese-Amerikan engineer, was being taken out for his traditional pre-wedding "bachelor party" by his friends that night in 1982.

They were happily drinking at a topless bar, watching Black and white women undress, when two blue-collar white men, thinking the party were the Japanese who had cost them their auto plant jobs, called Chin racist names. He got up and challenged them to a fight. But when he got outside, Chin discovered in horror that his fellow Amerikans weren't going to play fair. Chin ran away on foot, pursued by the two in their car. Unable to find help in his state, Chin was finally cornered and beaten to death.

The Asian-Amerikan movement got upset when a white Michigan judge expressed sympathy for the white defendants, and let them off with probation. A "Justice For Vincent Chin" committee was formed. There were protests, speeches, press conferences with Congress, the whole routine except for renting Al Sharpton. Years later in 1987 the murderer was retried on Federal Civil Rights violation charges—and acquitted. As he said happily, it was just a barroom fight that got blown out of proportion. End of case.

Do you know, the Asian-Amerikan movement still hasn't figured it out (the glory of integration is that former Third World people get to be as stupid as white men are). Hey, Vincent Chin already got justice. It wasn't nice, but it was just. If you want to be like white men, if you want to hang out in porno bars with them, if you want to get drunk and roll in the gutter with them—then it's on you. This isn't Mao we're talking about here—you gotta deal with the consequences of your own class-cultural choices. It won't be any other way, anyway, no matter how much someone complains about it.

Get real. Those protesting middle-class Asian-Amerikans weren't that upset. If they were, the millions of them would have brought some justice to that white settler, who wasn't exactly hiding out in Detroit there. Two young Chinese-Amerikan women film-makers even hung out for days with the killer in his home, doing an "anti-racist" documentary on him. If they were that upset, they could have pulled a .45 out of their camera bag and expressed him to redneck heaven (but no, they didn't have a grant for that).

The thing is, middle-class Asians wanted the government to do the hard part for them. That's their whole point, that protection should come from the oppressor—maybe in the mail like your credit card. When nothing happens, they say "it's racism." No, it's beyond racism. It's the *real* Multiculturalism. Listen up. It's just like when whites protest that they're being edged out of their customary goody positions by Asians or other immigrants—the government isn't even listening. Could care less.

Last year's freshman class at UCLA was 40% Asian, marking their replacement of euro-amerikans as the largest racial group (while the number of entering Black students was quietly cut in 1991 by 23%—Asians aren't protesting that, are they?). The University of California system as a whole is already 26% Asian, and everyone admits that in the 21st century whites are just going to be another minority there. Formerly white-majority City College of New York is so Third World now that the student Italian-American club has mostly Latin and West Indian members. This is the ticket to real jobs, the middle-class "union card" we're talking about. Whites are loudly whining about their kids being unfairly out-competed academically by hordes of "over-achiever" Asian students. And you know, imperialism doesn't care one way or the other. Increasingly, it's if little Whitey Jr. can't cut it, then later for him.

Under neo-colonialism, imperialism is going to lay back and let everybody, parasites included, fight it out. It has little alternative, really. If it took 500,000 U.S. bozos, NATO, Islamic men's armies, plus jet squadrons and a giant "U.N." naval fleet just to temporarily settle Iraq vs. Kuwait (two small artificial nations most folks never heard of before), how can imperialism simultaneously handle Corsicans vs. French, Sikhs vs. Hindus, Tutsi vs. Hutus, Sunni vs. Shiite, Canadians vs. Quebec, Clarence vs. Anita, and ten thousand other conflicts? And why should it? Do you know how many wars and rumbles there are right now?

No, they've given up trying to impose even their old-style order on the world, and are letting their nations and races and genders fight it out while they lay back in the cut and manipulate the chaos as profitably as possible. Unless it directly attacks their interests or de-stabilizes things too much, Imperialism is forcing everyone to go freestyle. This is the beat of the neo-colonial age.

It's all come as a big shock to the Civil Rights babies, to the generation who grew up after colonialism in amerikkka had been replaced by neo-colonialism—i.e. civil rights, integration, and equal opportunity.

White women are confused with our new Pandora benefit package. Along with our box of newly opened up career opportunities, is packed sexual harassment, women-hating violence of all kinds, rape and murders. This mixes up our synapses. We think, if we're getting political rights, equal opportunity, condos and all, then we assume we're supposed to get more protection and safety, too. But it's the reverse.

The ruling class program is that if you want to leave the harem and compete out there in the big world, then you have to take your chances with everyone else. If you can't defend yourself, then it's all on you. Big Daddy in Washington will go through the motions, but he really isn't going to hold your hand (which is what these white equal opportunity women really want, to have it both ways). Violent men get equal opportunity, too. It's the *real* Multiculturalism.

PARASITISM IS NEO-COLONIALISM

While there are many different nationalities, races and genders in the u.s., the supposedly different cultures in multi-culturalism don't like to admit what they have in common, the glue to it all—parasitism. Right now, there's both anger among the oppressed and a milling around, edging up to the next step but uncertain what it is fully, what it means. The key is the common need to break with parasitism. Which is a hard thing.

While recognition of Black Genocide is openers to being a player and not a pawn in amerikkkan politics, that alone is not sufficient to grasp what is in motion.

The most significant side of Black Genocide right now is the paradox of parasitism—of how many New Afrikan people have an individual and class interest in Black Genocide. Are dependent for their well-being on Black Genocide. To

understand anything scientifically, we have to see it as a paradox, an unfolding contradiction. In that light, it's pathetic
to hear old nationalists from the 1960s still talk that stuff
about "Black Unity", when it's precisely that unconscious
unity around wrong principles that prevents the Black
Nation from finding life or death answers, from saving itself.

You think those guys dealing drugs don't know they're
helping capitalism kill people off? They may be doomed, but
they're not out of it. What they say is "Hey, it's too bad, but
somebody's going to do it, so it might as well be me who
gets the 'benz and the Alpine." Yet and again, how's that
different from the "good" people with Master's degrees and
Mastercards, who might belong to NAACP, NOI, or Jacks
and Jills, whose home and cars in the suburbs comes from
being a supervisor in the social agency.

Maybe they're even worse, since they cry "urban crisis"
and talk that talk about "endangered species"—but only to
pressure for more government funding for their bureaucracy
(and capitalist welfare-type agencies can't be any answer,
since they're part of the problem). They aren't professionals in any way at stopping genocide—to name the precise
problem—but only professional at helping capitalism pretend to be doing something about its intensifying destruction. Intellectual crack.

Only different on the outside from those "angry" Hip-
Hop artists who know inside that the message they send out
is in part propaganda conditioning men to violently attack
Afrikan women. If you read up on your Malcolm, but now
rap about "fucked that bitch" and "made that pussy pay", you
know what you're doing even if you don't want to admit it.
But someone's going to get those big bucks for doing it, so
why not you? euro-capitalism can't very well have *white* men

do commercials urging the genocidal terrorism and repression of Black women and children, can they? No, gotta have some Black men do it. And if on the side you mix in some fast talk about shoot-outs with Porky or admiring Afro heroes, then you can claim to just be "angry." "Anger" is a neocolonial commodity now, too.

Point is, there are significant numbers of neo-colonized Afrikan-Amerikans today whose class interest is in going along with Black Genocide. Under neo-colonialism, their individual careers, interests and survival were unbundled from the common braid of their former colonized people. They're sorry about it, worried about it, but aren't going to fight their own "American" interests any more than the Jewish community in the u.s. was willing to risk its privileges to save those other Jews threatened by the Nazi Holocaust in the 1930s and 1940s. That's ugly, but true.

You can't say "Black Unity" as though things haven't changed. Folks used to say "Uncle Tom, the Preacher," but now it's "Uncle Tom, the Supreme Court Justice", "Uncle Tom, the Chairman of the Joint Chiefs of Staff", "Uncle Tom, the Police Chief." This is really a different situation, where capitalism is enrolling as citizens some of Afrikan descent while isolating many others for eventual extermination—all based on class.

A whole Afrikan-Amerikan capitalistic subculture has shot up, marked not only by tasting real money but by being so neo-colonized that it produces not a few folks too stupid to survive. Which is why you get star-fucker Desiree up in dim-witted Iron Mike's hotel room at 2 a.m. Two folks peddling their bodies and dignity for capitalism's show & tell games (some women think they shoulda put her moms on trial first). A young New Afrikan sister lives down the hall was saying one night how late it is for all these folks, not just Desiree and Mike but all the stupid hustlers and crimies, the dopeheads, who can't get it together. "Maybe,we'll have to just let them die out," she said. The oppressed have to break with parasitism—which means dis-unity with everyone who can't give up parasitism or won't. *By any means necessary.*

CHAPTER EIGHT:

OLD REALITY MORPHS INTO NEW REALITY

There is a restlessness among those who seek root change because we're at the turning point where an old reality is giving way to a new reality. Both are still present & true at one and the same time. Combining but increasingly colliding. Especially in our minds.

Home videotape allows the fascinated world to watch as a mob of white L.A. cops club & kick a Black man over and over into the hospital. Old reality. At the same time, amerikkka puts another Afrikan-Amerikan man in command of reorganizing its military. Its elite combat units in Panama & the Gulf War, such as the 82nd Airborne, are half-New Afrikan. In a resurge of white pride, the most requested video on MTV in 1991 is a Black woman widely rumored to be a lesbian singing a pop version of the white man's national anthem. New reality.

A car full of klansmen shoot a New Afrikan man in a drive by & three loser skinheads ambush gays and lesbians outside bars. Old reality. At the same time, NYC's Black mayor holds onto the headlines by helping Irish gays & lesbians crash the St. Paddy's day parade; marching with them at the rear, while white cops charge into the Fifth Ave. crowds to arrest white men hurling beer cans at the mayor. New reality.

We've seen pioneering hip hop group Run-DMC accused of anti-Semitism because of the mockingly stereotyped portrayal of a Jew in their movie—a movie deliberately so written, directed, and produced by their Jewish male business partner. "Black anti-semitism" is now another business, really. We've seen white lesbians joining city councils, on Wall St. corporate boards, even in the u.s. senate. New reality, ready or not.

While Black Genocide is shooting up in the backyard.

The old reality is *colonialism*, while the new reality is *neo-colonialism*. Not replacing or eliminating our old reality, but merging with it and taking it over.

The transformation to a neo-colonial world has only begun, but it promises to be as drastic, as disorienting a change as was the original european colonial conquest of the human race. Capitalism is again ripping apart & restructuring the world, and nothing will be the same. Not race, not nation, not gender, and certainly not whatever culture you used to have.

In this wrenching transformation, national empires, national borders & national economic rivalries are becoming less important to the international ruling class. To them, nations are less like the fortified bases of monopoly they used to be, but more like mere provinces, commercial suburbs, places of convenience for their multinational corporations. Nations are being subdivided, built & torn down at an increasing tempo by capitalist evolution itself. Nations aren't seen any more as fixed, eternal, god-given—which was all delusion—but as ambiguous and subject to the class struggle.

But when the oppressed call themselves a nation they mean freedom from imperialistic power and its involuntary nations to build their new culture, their own economy, a new try at civilization. For example, for their way of life to thrive, Indian peoples must have their First Nations—how can they survive if imperialism owns the land & sovereignty? Can you become a free people based on bingo games & being a tourist ghetto?

Many peoples were involuntarily submerged to make larger nations/empires (and in places like India and the late Soviet Union we see opportunistic politicians and stunted capitalistic classes scrambling to tap that popular feeling).

So the weakening role of nations in the neo-imperial economy, their becoming more porous & less under control with decolonization, is leading to more nations not fewer. And the rise of new concepts as well: of nations as voluntary choices for people; of nations as being forms for change not dead tradition.

Now you have outcast groups as diverse as the Aryan Nation and the Queer Nation and the Hip Hop Nation publicly rejecting the right of the u.s. government to rule them, as obsolete white amerikkka is not merely declining but starting to break up just like the ussr, Yugoslavia, Great Britain and India are already doing. In the future everyone, even fools, will be able to see it, but the righteous should be able to read the earthsigns now.

All the building blocks of human culture—race, gender, nation, and especially class—are being transformed under great pressure to embody the spirit of this neo-colonial age.

Millions upon millions are migrating across nations; across genders, too, if we want to admit it. The largest population transfers in human history, surpassing even the Atlantic slave trade. *How can it be the same again?* Look at the recent Brooklyn Crown Heights "race riot," where a

hasidic Jewish fascist from Israel runs a red light following
their chief's police bodyguard & kills an Afrikan child from
Guyana. In retaliation, some 15 year-old Afrikan child from
Trinidad allegedly stabs another hasidic man from Australia.
Then a few hundred Afrikan youth, many of whom are
from Jamaica, stone & attack police, as well as looting stores
owned by Arabs, Taiwanese, Koreans and other nationalities. Black children, who have no leaders and are out of
history, follow white people on the street chanting "Hitler!
Hitler!" Nothing is the same any more. Like that L.A. "riot,"
which was a New Afrikan thing, only the majority of the
looters arrested turned out to be Latinos.

The director of the film "El Norte" said: "There are hundreds of thousands of refugees from Central America in
Los Angeles alone. Nobody knows the exact number, but
a recent TV inquiry estimated 300,000 to 400,000. In our
own research, we came across a community of Mayans from
Guatemala—5,000 from *one* village—now in Los Angeles.
The original village, which is now dead, had 15,000."[98] Over
200 Indian villages totally disappeared during the 1980s
genocide in Guatemala, under the efficient supervision of
borrowed Israeli military officers.

Now you got entire Mayan villages hiding "underground"
in L.A. The thing is, they'll never be the same again. Not as
a race or a nation or a gender or a class. No, not after death
squads and final solutions, nintendo, birth control pills,
Slick Rick & student financial aid. They're not going back to
the farm again. In the same cities we got lesbian communities "underground", too. Lots of people *live* in amerikkka but
don't always think of themselves as "Americans."

In our zeal to expose imperialism's evil, its oppression, we
forgot that it is, to borrow a phrase, "wickedly great." That

capitalism can cause so much human suffering precisely because it is the most relentlessly revolutionary exploitative class society the earth has ever seen. The best-known passage in all political theory, written 150 years ago, sounds almost contemporary in describing the essential rhythm of this society:

> "The bourgeoisie cannot exist without constantly revolutionizing the instruments of production, and thereby the relations of production, and with them the whole relations of society. Conservation of the old modes of production in unaltered form, was, on the contrary, the first condition of existence for all earlier industrial classes. Constant revolutionizing of production, uninterrupted disturbance of all social conditions, everlasting uncertainty and agitation distinguish the bourgeois epoch from all earlier ones. All fixed, fast-frozen relations, with their train of ancient and venerable prejudices and opinions, are swept away, all newly formed ones become antiquated before they can ossify. All that is solid melts into air, all that is holy is profaned, and woman is at last compelled to face with sober senses, her real conditions of life, and her relations with her kind.

> "The need of a constantly expanding market for its products chases the bourgeoisie over the whole surface of the globe. It must nestle everywhere, settle everywhere, establish connexions everywhere.

> "The bourgeoisie has through its exploitation of the world-market given a cosmopolitan character

to production and consumption in every country. To the great chagrin of Reactionists, it has drawn from under the feet of industry the national ground on which it stood. All old-established national industries have been destroyed or are daily being destroyed. They are dislodged by new industries, whose introduction becomes a life and death question for all civilized nations, by industries that no longer work up indigenous raw material, but raw material drawn from the remotest zones; industries whose products are consumed, not only at home, but in every quarter of the globe. In place of the old wants, satisfied by the productions of the country, we find new wants, requiring for their satisfaction the products of distant lands and climes. In place of the old local and national seclusion and self-sufficiency, we have intercourse in every direction, universal inter-dependence of nations. And as in material, so also in intellectual production. The intellectual creations of individual nations become common property ... It compels all nations, on pain of extinction, to adopt the bourgeois mode of production; it compels them to introduce what it calls civilization into their midst, i.e., to become bourgeois themselves. In one word, it creates a world after its own image."[99]

Neo-colonialism, as the latest stage of capitalism, is realizing a process begun at the dawn of industrialization. At first, european capitalism replicated itself only among its "kith & kin." So 17th century Holland, a tiny nation but then a major european colonial power, promoted capitalism in England. England, in its turn, promoted capitalism in its white settler

colonies of amerikkka & Canada. Now, capitalism is repli-
cating itself indigenously in Asia, Afrika, Latin Amerika &
the Middle East. Led by the fading u.s. empire, which in the
1950s promoted the industrialization of Taiwan, South Korea
& Hong Kong alongside their re-industrialization of Japan.

Neo-colonialism (which literally means "new & different
colonialism") isn't merely colonialism fronted with David
Dinkins and Ann Richards, but a drastic overhaul of imperialism forced by both internal and external factors. Both the
victorious anti-colonial revolutions in colony after colony
during the years 1945–1975, and the evolution of the capitalist economy itself, gave birth to this change. We are now
experiencing the integration of former national capitalisms,
colonies & monopolies into one borderless world economy
(although to workers there are many borders) and one class
structure. A formally decolonized but unfree world.

Within the center of this change is the dialectic of con-
tinuity. We are living in a continuation of 18th and 19th
century industrial barbarism, only on a higher level of capitalist "civilization." The dispossessed and semi-slave proletariat of early european industry have never disappeared
at all, but have merely been displaced out of sight into the
Third World and the migrant Fourth World, multiplying
a thousand times and becoming the fastest growing class.
Capitalism's economic dependence on genocide and slavery,
which determined the content of its character during the
colonial era, still continues as the unseen foundation of the
imperial economy.

In these last few paragraphs we've laid down a quick and
very summarized overview of our analysis.

Everyone is looking for new political answers. Young
movements are groping for strategies & programs. We are

not even pretending to offer those answers, and it's important to understand why. Because new answers come from the grassroots, from the strategies and understandings that always arise out of the struggles of the oppressed themselves. From the inventions, trials and errors of practice. Whether it's the Black Panther Party or ACT-UP. The political answers we need are only going to come from new struggles, new social forces taking over.

This is not a blind or thoughtless process, however. The first step for anyone looking for answers is to know the situation. And that is what we are doing here, analyzing into the heart of the neo-colonial situation.

Out of this analysis three definite concepts emerge. Those who are really seeking root change have to detox ourselves from outmoded ideas—which may have been useful and on the mark just yesterday—and dysfunctional politics. *For we all need to take our part in dismantling the old structures within our political thinking.*

Secondly, we have to recognize that the reshaping of the neo-colonialized world in every instance reflects or is the result of, basic material changes in the system of economic production & distribution. Even the changer has been changed.

Finally, that the main contradiction for the oppressed is that of parasitism. The old anti-colonial unities of race or nation or gender are dysfunctional now, because the parasitic class relations of neo-colonialism have overridden everything. Parasitism is the knot that remains uncut awaiting new answers. Let us begin at the beginning, at the root of change.

STOP GENOCIDE

If you ever think about me and if you ain't gonna do no revolutionary act, forget about me. I don't want myself on your mind ... Let me say peace to you if you're willing to fight for it.

Fred Hampton
Chairperson, Illinois Black Panther Party

Born: August 30, 1948

Murdered by the f.b.i.
and the Chicago Police:

December 4, 1969

ENDNOTES

1. Rosemary Bray. "Recriminations Against Ourselves" *New York Times Magazine*. November 17, 1991.

2. "Text of Jeffries' July speech." *New York Newsday*. August 19, 1991. (complete text as transcribed from videotape).

3. Dr. Frances Cress Welsing, M.D. *The Issis (Ysts) Papers*. Chicago. 1991. pp. 232–233 (Third World Press).

4. Frantz Fanon. *The Wretched of the Earth*. N.Y. 1968. p. 40 (Grove Press).

5. James McPherson. "A Brief For Equality: the Abolitionist Reply to the Slavery Myth." In Martin Duberman, Ed. *The Anti-Slavery Vanguard*. N.Y. 1965. pp. 166–167 (Beacon Press).

6. James McPherson. "A Brief For Equality: the Abolitionist Reply to the Slavery Myth." In Martin Duberman, Ed. *The Anti-Slavery Vanguard*. N.Y. 1965. pp. 166–167 (Beacon Press).

7. Interview. *Washington Post*. December 3, 1991.

8. J. Sakai. *Settlers: The Mythology of the White Proletariat from Mayflower to Modern*. 4th edition. Kersplebedeb (Montreal/Oakland, 2014), pp. 147–8.

9. Attributed by Herman Rauschning. Quoted in: Robert C.L. Waite *Vanguard of Nazism*. N.Y. 1969 p. 131.

10. Sakai. pp. 16–18.

11. Sakai, pp. 5–6.

12. Sakai. pp. 15–16.

13. Sakai. pp. 10–12.

14. Emile Zola. *Germinal*. N.Y. 1970. p. 14 and p. 104.

15. Zola. p. 35

16. Zola. p. 37

17. Eric Williams. *Capitalism and Slavery*. N.Y. 1966. pp. 102–103

18. "The Role of Women & Children in the Armed Struggle." In *Bottomfish Blues*. No. 4 Summer 1989. Reprinted as the book *The Military Strategy of Women and Children* (Kersplebedeb, 2003), pp. 10–28.

19. *Washington Post*. August 31, 1990.

20. Kwame Nkrumah. *Revolutionary Path*. N.Y. 1973 pp. 310–314 (International Publishers).

21. Kwame Nkrumah. *Neo-Colonialism: the last stage of imperialism*. N.Y. 1970 p. ix (International Publishers).

22. David Rodney. *Kwame Nkrumah: the political kingdom in the Third World*. N.Y. 1989 pp. 248–253 (Oxford).

23. Fanon p. 70. Also see: Ambassade De France. "First Elections Under Universal Suffrage Held in Black Afrika, a Decisive Step Towards Self-Government." *African Affairs*. no.18 N.Y. May 1957.

24. Patrick Chabal. *Amilcar Cabral: Revolutionary leadership and peoples war*. Cambridge 1983. pp. 172–175.

25. Amilcar Cabral. "Brief Analysis of the Social Structure in Guinea." *In Revolution in Guinea*. N.Y. 1969 p. 71.

26. Amilcar Cabral. "The Weapon of Theory." In *Unity & Struggle*. N.Y. 1979 p. 133.

27. Cabral. "Brief Analysis …" p. 69.

28. Cabral. "Weapon of Theory." p. 136.

29. "Pseudo-Gangs." *S1*. June, 1983.

30. C.L.R.. James *Nkrumah & the Ghana Revolution*. Westport. 1977. p. 131.

31. James. pp. 55–56.

32. T. Peter Omari. *Kwame Nkrumah: the anatomy of an Afrikan dictatorship*. N.Y. 1970 p. 38.

33. Elisabeth Croll. *Feminism and Socialism in China*. (Routledge & Kegan Paul.) London. 1978.

34. Edith Thomas. *The Women Incendiaries*. N.Y. 1966 (George Braziller Inc.).

35. "Women & Children in the Armed Struggle." *Bottomfish Blues*. No.6. 1993. An edited version of these articles was published as *The Military Struggle of Women and Children* (Kersplebedeb, 2003).

36. Karl Marx quoted in Bertell Ollman. *Alienation*. N.Y. 1977. p. 64.

37. Robert B. Reich. *The Work of Nations*. N.Y. 1991. p. 8.

38. Stephen Labaton, "The cost of Drug Abuse: $60 Billion a Year." *New York Times*. December 5, 1989.

39. Stephen Labaton, "The cost of Drug Abuse: $60 Billion a Year." *New York Times*. December 5, 1989.

40. Stephen Labaton, "The cost of Drug Abuse: $60 Billion a Year." *New York Times*. December 5, 1989.

41. The Hunger Project. *Ending Hunger: an idea whose time has come*. N.Y. 1985. p. 219.

42. *New York Times*. June 7, 1989 *Moody's International Manual*. Vol. I. N.Y. 1986.

43. James Petras. "Chile's Exploited Farm Workers." *Christian Science Monitor*. April 11, 1989.

44. The Hunger Project. p. 233

45. Karl Marx. "Wage, Labor and Capital." In *Selected Works*. N.Y. 1970 p. 81.

46. *New York Times*. April 17, 1988.

47. *New York Times*. May 12, 1988.

48. Ibid.

49. *New York Times*. February 23, 1992.

50. *Washington Post*. March 31, 1992.

51. *New York Times*. March 30, 1989.

52. A. Sivanadan. "Imperialism in the Silicon Age." *Monthly Review*. July–August. 1980

53. Glen Rifkin. "High Tops, High Style, High Tech, High Cost." *New York Times*. January 5, 1992

54. Karl Marx. *Capital, a critique of political economy.* Vol I. Chicago. 1921. p. 836 (Charles H. Kerr & Co.).

55. David E. Sanger. "Cost May Be Too High For All-American Chip." *New York Times.* January 1, 1992.

56. A. Sivanadan. op. cit.

57. Louis Uchitelle. "U.S. Businesses Loosen Links to Mother Country." *New York Times.* May 21, 1989.

58. Ibid.

59. NBC Nightly News. April 13, 1992.

60. Louis Uchitelle. "U.S. Businesses Loosen Links to Mother Country." *New York Times.* May 21, 1989.

61. Gavin Wright. "Beyond Economic Nationalism." *Washington Post.* March 3, 1992.

62. Frank H. Wu. "The Fallout from Japan-Bashing." *Washington Post.* February 3, 1992.

63. "U.S. Businesses Start Counterattacks in Japan." *New York Times.* February 24, 1992.

64. A. Sivanadan. op. cit.

65. Robert Andersen. "An Anthology of the World." *New York Times* Book Review.

66. Samir Amin. "The Class Structure of the Contemporary World." *Monthly Review.* January. 1980.

67. Christopher Hill. *The Making of Modern English Society. Vol. I. Reformation to Industrial Revolution. 1530–1780.* N.Y. 1967. pp. 215–216

68. Ibid.

69. Karl Marx. *Capital*. Vol. I. N.Y. 1967 p. 761 (International Publishers).

70. Hill pp. 64–65.

71. *Capital*. Vol I. N.Y. 1967 pp. 394–397.

72. *Capital*. pp. 759–760.

73. See: Raya Dunayevskaya. *Rosa Luxemburg. Women's Liberation & Marx's Philosophy of Revolution*. Urbana 1991 (University of Illinois Press).

74. T.O. Ranger. "The Nineteenth Century in Southern Rhodesia." In *Southern African Politics*. N.Y. 1967. pp. 113–114.

75. Salim Lone. "Afterward, Make Africa A Priority." *New York Times*. February 3, 1991.

76. Jonathan P. Hicks. "Study Shows U.S. Reliance on South African Metals." *New York Times*. August 25, 1985.

77. Malcolm W. Browne. "Fearing Instability, West Seeks to Replace Minerals From South Africa." *New York Times*. July 15, 1986.

78. James Brooke. "Used U.S. Clothes a Bestseller in Africa." *New York Times*. February 16, 1987.

79. Browne. op. cit.

80. *Capital*. Vol I. p. 246.

81. Bill Tarrant. "Millions of children live as 'slaves' in Asia." *Washington Times*. July 14, 1989.

82. Joseph Albright & Marcial Kunstel. "Child Labor: the Profits of Shame." *Washington Post.* July 12, 1987.

83. "UNICEF Official Quits Amid Sex Scandal." Reuters dispatch. *The Sun.* June 24, 1987.

84. Joseph Albright & Marcial Kunstel. "Child Labor: the Profits of Shame." *Washington Post.* July 12, 1987.

85. Alan Riding. "Brazil's Burgeoning Arms Industry." *New York Times.* November 3, 1985.

86. Alan Riding. "For Brazilian, U.S. Trip Marks Surge in Status." *New York Times.* September 7, 1986.

87. Maruse Simons. "Brazil Health Crisis..." *New York Times.* February 13, 1987.

88. Cynthia Enloe. *Bananas, Beaches & Bases.* Berkeley 1990. p. 160 (University California Berkeley Press).

89. Cynthia Enloe. *Bananas, Beaches & Bases.* Berkeley 1990. p. 168 (University California Berkeley Press).

90. Jack Miles. "Black vs. Browns." *Atlantic Monthly.* October 1992.

91. Robert D. Hershey, Jr. "U.S. Study Finds Nearly 3 out of 10 Get Benefits." *New York Times.* September 27, 1984.

92. Howe & Longman. Op. cit.

93. Barbara Vobejda. "In Job Strength, Manufacturing Eclipsed by Public Sector." *Washington Post.* August 18, 1992.

94. James Bovard. "Stop Coddling Farmers." *New York Times.* January 16, 1985.

95. WCBS-TV Nightly News. July 10,1987.

96. CBS Evening News. July 10, 1987.

97. Alison Mitchell. "Illegal Vans in Battle for New York's Streets." *New York Times*. January 24, 1992.

98. Interview *New York Times*. January 8, 1984.

99. Karl Marx & Frederick Engels. "Communist Manifesto" in *Selected Works*. N.Y. 1970. pp. 40–41 (International Publishers).

SELECTED BIBLIOGRAPHY

Beck, Emilia, Morris & Patterson. "Strike One To Educate
    One Hundred": the rise of the Red Brigades in Italy in
    the 1960s–1970s. Chicago. 1986.

Bertolt Brecht. Mother Courage & Her Children. N.Y. 1987.

Bottomfish Blues. Amazon Nation or Aryan Nation: White
    Women and the Coming of Black Genocide. Montreal.
    2014.
———— Bottomfish Blues: a voice for the amazon nation.

Bromma. Exile and Reconstruction: Working Class Women
    at the Heart of Globalization. Montreal. 2014.
———— The Worker Elite. Montreal. 2014.

Amilcar Cabral. Unity & Struggle: speeches and writings.
    N.Y. 1979.

Jimmie Durham. American Indian Culture: traditionalism &
    spiritualism in a revolutionary struggle. Chicago. 1983.

Cynthia Enloe. Bananas, Beaches & Bases: making feminist
    sense of international politics. Berkeley. 1990.

Frantz Fanon. The Wretched of the Earth. N.Y. 1968.

Leslie Feinberg. Stone Butch Blues. Ithaca. 1993.

Paula Giddings. When and Where I Enter: the impact of
    Black women on race and sex in America. N.Y. 1985.

Claudia Koonz. Mothers in the Fatherland. N.Y. 1987.

Butch Lee. Jailbreak out of History: The Rebiography of
    Harriet Tubman, and "The Evil of Female Loaferism".
    Montreal. 2015.

———— *The Military Strategy of Women and Children.*
Montreal 2003.

Audre Lorde. *Zami: a new spelling of my name.* N.Y. 1982.

Karl Marx. *Capital. Vol. 1. The Process of Capitalistic
Production.* Chicago. 1921.

Maria Mies. *Patriarchy and Accumulation on a World Scale:
women in the international division of labor.* London.
1986.
———— "Capitalist Development and Subsistence
Reproduction; Rural Women in India." *Journal of
Concerned Asian Scholars.* January–March 1980.
(subsequently included as a chapter in her book, *Last
Colony*)

Pat Parker. *Movement in Black; the collected poetry of Pat
Parker 1961–1978.* Ithaca. 1989.

Rayna R. Reiter. ed. *Toward an Anthropology of Women.*
N.Y. 1976.

Walter Rodney. *How Europe Underdeveloped Africa.* (rev.
ed.) Washington. 1982.
———— *Walter Rodney Speaks.* Trenton. 1990.

J. Sakai. *Settlers: The Mythology of the White Proletariat from
Mayflower to Modern.* Montreal/Oakland. 2014.

James Yaki Sayles. *Meditations on Frantz Fanon's Wretched
of the Earth: New Afrikan Revolutionary Writings.*
Montreal. 2010.

Agnes Smedley. *The Great Road: the life & times of Chu Teh.*
N.Y. 1972.

Valerie Solanas. *S.C.U.M. Manifesto*. N.Y. 1967.

Edith Thomas. *The Women Incendiaries*. English
    Translation George Braziller Inc. 1966

Christina Thurmer-Rohr. *Vagabonding: Feminist thinking
    cut loose*. Boston. 1991.

Judith Van Allen. "'Aha Riots' or Igbo 'Women's War'?
    Ideology, Stratification, and the Invisibility of
    Women." in Nancy J. Hafkin & Edna G. Bay. *Women
    In Africa*. Stanford. 1976.

Nym Wales & Kim San. *Song of Ariran: a Korean
    communist in the Chinese revolution*. Forrestville. 1973.

Amazon Nation or Aryan Nation: White Women and the Coming of Black Genocide

Bottomfish Blues
9781894946551
168 pages
$12.95

The two main essays, "Kill the Kids First" and "Integration," first appeared in the underground Amazon newspaper Bottomfish Blues in the 1980s. These essays show how the massive New Afrikan uprisings of the 1960s were answered by the white ruling class: with the destruction of New Afrikan communities coast to coast, the decimation of the New Afrikan working class, the rise of the prison state and an explosion of violence between oppressed people. Taken on their own, in isolation, these blights may seem to be just more "social issues" for NGOs to get grants for, but taken together and in the context of amerikkkan history, they constitute genocide.

A third essay, "The Ideas of Black Genocide in the Amerikkkan Mind" was first circulated in 2009; it recounts how the idea of Black Genocide has always been present in the u.s., from the 1700s onward.

SIMILAR BOOKS FROM KERSPLEBEDEB LEFTWINGBOOKS.NET
KERSPLEBEDEB CP 63560, CCCP VAN HORNE, MONTREAL, QUEBEC, CANADA, H3W 3H8

The Military Strategy of Women and Children

Butch Lee

0973143231

116 pages

$12.00

The Military Strategy of Women and Children lays out the need for an autonomous and independent women's revolutionary movement, a revolutionary women's culture that involves not only separating oneself from patriarchal imperialism, but also in confronting, opposing, and waging war against it by all means necessary.

The three main essays in this book appeared in slightly different form in the 1980s in the underground feminist newspaper Bottomfish Blues, while the postscript ("There's Fighting in Iraq but the Real Women'sWar is in Afrika") was written in 2003. They are the first parts of an ongoing work in progress—part four is published separately in the book Jailbreak Out of History.

SIMILAR BOOKS FROM KERSPLEBEDEB LEFTWINGBOOKS.NET
KERSPLEBEDEB CP 63560, CCCP VAN HORNE, MONTREAL, QUEBEC, CANADA, H3W 3H8

Jailbreak out of History:
The Rebiography
of Harriet Tubman,
& The "Evil of Female Loaferism"

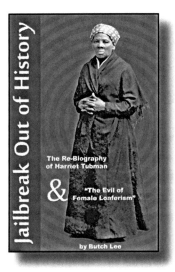

Butch Lee
9781894946704
169 pages
$14.95

Anticolonial struggles of New Afrikan/Black women were central to the unfolding of 19th century amerika, both during and "after" slavery. "The Re-Biography of Harriet Tubman" recounts the life and politics of Harriet Tubman, who waged and eventually lead the war against the capitalist slave system. "The Evil of Female Loaferism" details New Afrikan women's attempts to withdraw from and evade capitalist colonialism, an unofficial but massive labor strike which threw the capitalists North and South into a panic. The ruling class response consisted of the "Black Codes", Jim Crow, re-enslavement through prison labor, mass violence, and ... the establishment of a neo-colonial Black patriarchy, whose task was to make New Afrikan women subordinate to New Afrikan men just as New Afrika was supposed to be subordinate to white amerika.

SIMILAR BOOKS FROM KERSPLEBEDEB LEFTWINGBOOKS.NET
KERSPLEBEDEB CP 63560, CCCP VAN HORNE, MONTREAL, QUEBEC, CANADA, H3W 3H8

Meditations on Frantz Fanon's Wretched of the Earth:
New Afrikan Revolutionary Writings

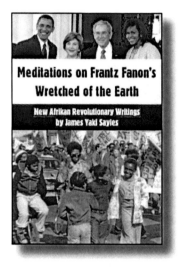

James Yaki Sayles

9781894946322

399 pages

$20.00

One of those who eagerly picked up Fanon in the '60s, who carried out armed expropriations and violence against white settlers, Sayles reveals how, behind the image of Fanon as race thinker, there is an underlying reality of antiracist communist thought.

"This exercise is about more than our desire to read and understand Wretched (as if it were about some abstract world, and not our own); it's about more than our need to understand (the failures of) the anti-colonial struggles on the African continent. This exercise is also about us, and about some of the things that We need to understand and to change in ourselves and our world."
—James Yaki Sayles

Settlers: The Mythology of the White Proletariat from Mayflower to Modern

J. Sakai

9781629630373

456 pages

$20.00

J. Sakai shows how the United States is a country built on the theft of Indigenous lands and Afrikan labor, on the robbery of the northern third of Mexico, the colonization of Puerto Rico, and the expropriation of the Asian working class, with each of these crimes being accompanied by violence. In fact, America's white citizenry have never supported themselves but have always resorted to exploitation and theft, culminating in acts of genocide to maintain their culture and way of life. This movement classic lays it all out, taking us through this painful but important history.

SIMILAR BOOKS FROM KERSPLEBEDEB LEFTWINGBOOKS.NET
KERSPLEBEDEB CP 63560, CCCP VAN HORNE, MONTREAL, QUEBEC, CANADA, H3W 3H8

KER
SPL
EBE
DEB

Since 1998 Kersplebedeb has been an important source of radical literature and agit prop materials.

The project has a non-exclusive focus on anti-patriarchal and anti-imperialist politics, framed within an anticapitalist perspective. A special priority is given to writings regarding armed struggle in the metropole, and the continuing struggles of political prisoners and prisoners of war.

The Kersplebedeb website presents historical and contemporary writings by revolutionary thinkers from the anarchist and communist traditions.

Kersplebedeb can be contacted at:

Kersplebedeb
CP 63560
CCCP Van Horne
Montreal, Quebec
Canada
H3W 3H8

email: info@kersplebedeb.com
web: www.kersplebedeb.com
         www.leftwingbooks.net

Kersplebedeb

CPSIA information can be obtained
at www.ICGtesting.com
Printed in the USA
LVOW07s0217071117
555199LV00007B/703/P